Anti-Ballistic Missile: Yes or No?

Anti-Ballistic Missile: Yes or No?

*A Special Report from the Center
for the Study of Democratic Institutions*

Introduction by Hubert H. Humphrey
Epilogue by William O. Douglas

ⓌⒷ HILL AND WANG   New York

STANDARD BOOK NUMBER (CLOTHBOUND EDITION): 8090–2710–0
STANDARD BOOK NUMBER (PAPERBACK EDITION): 8090–1351–7
LIBRARY OF CONGRESS CATALOGUE CARD NUMBER: 73–77878

First edition April 1969

Composed, printed, and bound by Kingsport Press, Inc., Kingsport, Tennessee

Grateful acknowledgment is made for the use of copyrighted material from the following sources:
"Remarks by Secretary of Defense Robert S. McNamara, September 18, 1967," Bulletin of the Atomic Scientists (December, 1967).
"A Glossary of Strategic Weaponry" and "Congress and the Evolution of the ABM," Congressional Digest, Vol. 47, No. 11 (November, 1968).
Selections from the CQ Fact Sheet "On Sentinel System," Congressional Quarterly, Vol. 26, No. 36 (September 6, 1968).
Jeremy Stone, The Case Against Missile Defences, Adelphi Paper No. 47 (April, 1968), The Institute for Strategic Studies.
The Military Balance—1968–1969, The Institute for Strategic Studies.

The Center for the Study of Democratic Institutions is an independent, private, nonprofit, educational institution devoted to the clarification, through dialogue, of basic issues confronting a democratic society.

At the Center, located in Santa Barbara, California, some twenty Senior Fellows—with professional backgrounds in a wide range of academic disciplines—convene almost daily to engage in dialogue with one another and with noted visitors from throughout the world.

Those sessions, recorded, along with written works resulting from them, are the basis of the Center's communications program—thousands of audio tapes for radio broadcast and *The Center Magazine* and Occasional Papers, published regularly for the Center membership.

The Center receives no funds from government, industry, or large foundations. It is supported by tax-deductible contributions from its individual members, who number more than 85,000.

President of the Center is Robert M. Hutchins, former President of the University of Chicago. Its legal entity is the Fund for the Republic, Inc.

Contents

vii

Jacoby, Leon W. Johnson, George S. McGovern, I. I. Rabi, H. Franz Schurmann, Harvey Wheeler, Jerome B. Wiesner

PREFACE
Donald McDonald

Since the end of World War II the nuclear arms relationship between the United States and Soviet Russia has been marked by calculation and miscalculation, many alarms, occasional accommodations, slowdowns, speed-ups, relative stabilization, much unease, and constant uncertainty, with the whole periodically subjected—especially during Presidential election campaigns—to misleading rhetoric about bomber gaps, missile gaps, and security gaps.

For more than a decade the two great powers, and perforce the rest of the world, have predicated their strategy upon a power balance based on what is popularly called deterrence, which is more precisely identified by scientists and military planners as "mutual assured destruction." That is, both the United States and Russia possess "second-strike" capability: If either is attacked, it can retaliate with sufficient force to inflict "unacceptable damage" on the other.

Until very recently this second-strike capability has been presumed to be an adequate safeguard against either power's initiating or provoking a nuclear attack. Both have acted on the premise that their offensive strength also provides a basis for defense strategy: Rational men would not attack in the face of certain knowledge that a nuclear exchange would be suicidal.

However, the era of deterrence has been marked by curious anomalies, usually arising from a nervous misreading of the other side's activities and intentions. Both great powers have amassed enough thermonuclear warheads to devastate most of the habitable world several times over, and in the process the United States has built up a four-to-one numerical superiority over Russia in the number of deliverable thermonuclear missiles. This ratio probably will increase dramatically when the United States' MIRV (multiple independently targetable reentry vehicles) and Poseidon (multiple warheads fitted to Polaris submarine-launched missiles) are fully deployed and operational. MIRV and Poseidon make it possible for one missile to carry from three to ten thermonuclear warheads, which can be detached in trajectory and aimed at as many separate targets.

Still, the offensive balance continues to hold. Although the United States has *numerical* superiority over Russia, this is not the same as *nuclear* superiority. Nuclear superiority is the power of one nation to inflict on another a first strike of such force that the other is not able to retaliate and inflict unacceptable damage on the attacker. Neither the United States nor Russia possesses such power. And William Foster, the Johnson Administration's director of the Arms Control and Disarmament Agency, said last fall that the "most authoritative experts have assured us" that neither side "can hope to attain [nuclear superiority] in the foreseeable future."

Although Russia and the United States have continued to pin their primary strategy on the deterrent power of their massive second-strike nuclear capability, this strategy has not precluded sporadic efforts on both sides to explore the possibilities of an active missile defense system. The immediate objective, to reduce casualties, is enormously attractive in its own right. The larger consideration is strategic: An anti-ballistic-missile defense system (ABM) that could nullify a substantial portion of the enemy's striking capability could reverse the balance of offensive power.

The record of such explorations has not been brilliant. In the 1950's, the United States spent thirty billion dollars on bomber defenses that later were found to have been full of holes. In the 1960's, the United States spent another twenty billion dollars on anti-ballistic-missile research and development but in every instance abandoned emerging defensive systems when it became obvious that, years before they could be deployed, the hardware and controls would have been rendered obsolescent by Russian offensive missile advances.

Despite these failures, pro-ABM pressure has continued to mount in opposition to official policy. Scientific advisers to three successive Presidents have opposed anti-missile expenditures, as did former Defense Secretary Robert McNamara, who served both Presidents Kennedy and Johnson. Then, a little more than a year ago, Secretary McNamara yielded. The background of this historic modification of ABM policy has been summarized by Jeremy Stone in an *Adelphi* report published by the British Institute for Strategic Studies:

On 18 September 1967, Mr. Robert S. McNamara, then US Secretary of Defense, announced plans to deploy a limited ballistic missile defence system (called Sentinel) against the possibility of an attack by Chinese ballistic missiles. He acted under considerable political pressure, and called the case for the weapon system "marginal." This political pressure was generated very largely by the belief—now thought to be mistaken—that the Soviet Union was deploying ballistic missile defences around far more than Moscow.

The Soviet Government had expressed willingness in principle to discuss limits on the arms race, but had delayed in setting a date for talks to begin. Many drew the conclusion that the Russians were "stealing a march" on the United States. Because this pressure combined with the problem of missile defence against China, and because China became the rationale for the decision taken, it is a decision almost impossible to reverse on the grounds of faulty American estimates of Soviet intentions. Indeed, the new US Secretary of Defense, Mr. Clark Clifford, has advised the Senate Armed Services Committee that he is for maintaining a "clear-cut nuclear supremacy" over the Soviet Union; this approach, distinctly more favourable to missile defence procurement than that of Mr. Mc-Namara, suggests an increase in the likelihood that the United States will press on to build a larger system. . . .

For eight years preceding the September 1967 decision to deploy a "thin" ballistic missile defence, United States Administrations considered and rejected suggestions that ongoing development programs for missile defence be followed by procurement of one system or another. At first it was a primitive Nike-Zeus missile—considered successful if it could make an "intercept" of a single incoming warhead. Such a system could have been built by 1963–64 but would, according to estimates made by the Defense Department in 1962, have been obsolete by the time it became operational. A more advanced system, Nike-X, could have been ordered in 1963 and built by 1968, but—relative to projected Soviet improvements—would have been obsolete by 1966.

These systems depended upon tracking incoming objects despite clouds of "chaff," then distinguishing between decoys and weapons, and then launching anti-missiles at located warheads. Since observations of atmospheric drag on incoming objects were critical to distinguishing them, the defence was required to wait until the attacking warhead had entered well into the atmosphere and to intercept perhaps 5,000 to 100,000 feet off the ground; hence it had to rely upon interceptors that could climb thousands of feet in a few seconds. For this reason also, it had to anticipate low-level detonation of adversary warheads, and hence it had to complement the system with fallout shelters. Finally, the defence was local in character, covering ranges of only 15 to 25 miles, and all but the largest 25 or 50 urban areas would have been undefended.

Although the systems under development were quite obviously improving throughout the 1959–65 period, they seemed, paradoxically, ever less likely to be built. The problem of civil defence, the partial coverage provided by the defence, the rising cost of building an ever more complicated system, a growing willingness to rely upon the balance of terror, the prospect of suitable Soviet penetration devices, a wide-spread desire not to stir up the arms race, and Mr. McNamara's emphasis on cost-effectiveness—all combined to limit the prospects for missile defence procurement.

In 1964, Communist China exploded her first bomb, and American strategists saw a threat that might be neutralized with greater confidence than could that of the Soviet Union. Not long thereafter, the range of the American interceptor missiles was greatly expanded. At the same time, new techniques were developed to permit the destruction of incoming missiles with X-rays while they were still outside the atmosphere. (Earlier systems had relied on blast effects in the atmosphere, and hence such systems were ineffective at airless altitudes.) The increased range of the interceptor, in conjunction with the new X-ray method of "kill," enormously improved paper-and-pencil calculations of effectiveness. Incoming missiles could be attacked several hundred miles up. Each interceptor battery could cover a ground radius of about 400 miles. When these results were considered with respect to the new (and weaker) prospective Chinese threat, some began to talk of the possibility of preventing any Chinese missiles from penetrating until the 1980's—even of discouraging China from building long-range missiles at all.

In this supersaturated situation, in 1966, some evidence was uncovered that the Soviet Union had begun to build a ballistic missile defence. Earlier sporadic Soviet efforts to build a single battery around Leningrad in 1962 had created only a stir. Now it seemed certain that a defensive system had been installed around Moscow. Elsewhere, unquestionably, something was being built rapidly. This more comprehensive installation (called the Tallinn system, after the Estonian city that housed part of it) was thought by some to be a defence against missiles. General Earle G. Wheeler testified that it would violate "military logic" if it were not. But despite an earlier news conference in which Mr. McNamara announced "considerable evidence" that the Soviet Union was deploying an anti-missile system, he testified in 1967 that existing evidence could be explained by the hypothesis of an extensive new air defence system. Presumably such a system would have been started in anticipation of a high-flying B-70, or it might have reflected compulsive vested interests in air defence. By 1968, a "majority" of Department of Defense analysts subscribed to Mr. McNamara's "air defence" view, and the situation was seen as follows in [testimony supporting] the fiscal 1969 defence budget:

"Now, I can tell you that the majority of our intelligence community no longer believes that this so-called 'Tallinn' system (which is being deployed across the northwestern approaches to the Soviet Union and in several other places) has any significant ABM capability. This system is apparently designed for use within the atmosphere, most likely against an aerodynamic rather than a ballistic missile threat.

"Although construction of the Galosh ABM system around Moscow is proceeding at a moderate pace, no effort has been made during the last year to expand that system or extend it to other cities. It is the consensus of the intelligence community that this system could provide a limited defence of the Moscow area but that it could be seriously degraded by sophisticated penetration aids."

Notwithstanding this new appraisal of Soviet plans, the Defense Department has not changed its own plans, asserting: "Nevertheless, knowing what we do about past Soviet predilections for defensive systems, we must, for the time being, plan our forces on the assumption that they will have deployed some sort of an ABM system around their major cities by the early 1970's." The phrase "for the time being" presumably refers to the possibility of American-Soviet discussions and may suggest American willingness to compromise in the presence of talks.

This shift in Defense Department policy, followed by Congressional authorization of the five-billion-dollar "thin" screen, has opened the way for ABM proponents to raise the ante and argue openly for the "thick" or "heavy" system, of which the Sentinel system would be simply the precursor and building-block. The initial cost of the ABM as now visualized is generally conceded to be in the range of forty to fifty billion dollars, and its scope has been escalated to provide protection for twenty-five to fifty American cities and for our missile-launching installations.

The debate between pro- and anti-ABM partisans has waxed in the sixteen months since Mr. McNamara's Sentinel announcement, in a curious and prophetic speech, in which he warned of the pressures that would follow:

There is a kind of mad momentum intrinsic to the development of all new nuclear weaponry. If a weapon system works—and works well—there is strong pressure from many directions to produce and deploy the weapon out of all proportion to the prudent level required.

The danger in deploying this relatively light and reliable Chinese-oriented ABM system is going to be that pressures will develop to expand it into a heavy Soviet-oriented ABM system.

We must resist that temptation firmly—not because we can for a moment afford to relax our vigilance against a possible Soviet first strike—but precisely because our greatest deterrent against such a strike is not a massive, costly, but highly penetrable ABM shield, but rather a fully credible offensive assured destruction capability.

The so-called heavy ABM shield—at the present state of technology—would in effect be no adequate shield at all against

a Soviet attack, but rather a strong inducement for the Soviets
to vastly increase their own offensive forces. That, as I have
pointed out, would make it necessary for us to respond in
turn—and so the arms race would rush hopelessly on to no
sensible purpose on either side.

The ABM debate has only incidentally involved the Sentinel
system as such. The Sentinel decision has been taken, Congress
has appropriated the construction funds, and presumably Sentinel will be deployed unless the new President, Mr. Nixon,
presses for a reversal of prevailing Defense Department policy.
But the debate over the basics of anti-ballistic-missile defense
is by no means over. The current round turns on whether a
heavy ABM system can be justified. The Sentinel decision did
not settle that argument; it only inflamed it. Mr. McNamara's
pronouncements before leaving office, and Secretary Clifford's
since assuming it, have done nothing to resolve the technical,
military, economic, and political differences that lie at the heart
of the ABM controversy.

Yet, despite the high status of the adversaries and the fateful
character of the issue, the ABM question has been debated in
rather restricted circles to date: in the scientific community,
before a few Congressional committees and on one occasion
before a secret session of the Senate as a whole, and in some
journals of opinion. In fragmented fashion the running controversy occasionally breaks through in the mass media, producing a prevailing editorial uneasiness among the more serious
newspapers, periodicals, and television commentators. And the
ABM issue turns up as a priority item on the agenda of all of
those concerned with the current state of international relations,
for it is well on the way to becoming the most immediate and
dangerous symptom of the Cold War.

To examine the current state of the ABM issue and appraise
its possible consequences, the Center for the Study of Democratic Institutions has brought together leading experts repre-

senting opposing scientific, military, and political views. Gathered in New York in late November, with the confusions and alarms of the Presidential election behind them, protagonists and antagonists of the ABM met in two lengthy sessions, the second of which broadened the discussion to include associates of the Center and others specially qualified to introduce subsidiary but essential political, economic, and social questions that flow from the central strategic issue. This publication is a distillation of those discussions and of the position papers prepared for them.

Two distinguished scientists with long experience in the development of nuclear weapons and with full access to classified defense information led off for and against the ABM. The looming thick anti-missile defense was supported as essential to the national security by Donald G. Brennan, former President of the Hudson Institute. It was attacked as worthless and potentially dangerous by Jerome B. Wiesner, Provost of Massachusetts Institute of Technology and former science advisor to President Kennedy. Dr. Brennan was given full support by General Leon W. Johnson (USAF retired), and Dr. Wiesner was backed by Senator George S. McGovern of South Dakota, the leading Congressional critic of the ABM. These principal position papers were delivered and briefly discussed at an evening session presided over by the Chairman of the Center's Board, Associate Justice William O. Douglas of the U.S. Supreme Court. "The Case Against the ABM" and "The Case for the ABM" are edited versions of those statements.

The following morning the antagonists met in a closed session to tape record their second thoughts and to enter into a free-ranging discussion with nine others who were either associated with the Center or invited because their special competence would insure a full range of relevant points of view. Those so met were:

Harry S. Ashmore, Executive Vice President, Center for the Study of Democratic Institutions.

Adolf A. Berle, Professor of Law at Columbia University, former Assistant Secretary of State, and a Center consultant.

Freeman Dyson, theoretical physicist, Institute for Advanced Study, Princeton, consultant to the Department of Defense.

W. H. Ferry, Vice President of the Center.

Charles M. Herzfeld, Technical Director, Defense Space Group, International Telephone and Telegraph Corporation.

Neil H. Jacoby, former Dean, Graduate School of Business Administration, University of California, Los Angeles, member of President Eisenhower's Council of Economic Advisers, and a Visiting Fellow of the Center.

I. I. Rabi, Nobel laureate, University Professor of Physics, Columbia University, and a Center consultant.

H. Franz Schurmann, Professor of History and Sociology and former Director of the Center for Chinese Studies at the University of California, Berkeley.

Harvey Wheeler, Fellow of the Center, author of *Fail-Safe* and *Democracy in a Revolutionary Era*.

Their exchanges are represented in the Colloquy section, which has been edited to point up the main topics developed in the course of several hours of discussion. Justice Douglas' summary observations are contained in the concluding essay "Why Not Try the Rule of Law?" The Appendixes contain essential background materials, including excerpts from papers submitted for the Center conference, the edited text of the September 18, 1967, announcement by former Defense Secretary Robert McNamara on deployment of the thin ABM system, a representative sampling of statements made in the course of Congressional consideration of the issue, a chronology of events leading to the present state of ABM development, and a glossary.

This special report by the Center for the Study of Democratic Institutions is introduced by Hubert H. Humphrey, former Vice President of the United States. A leader in arms-control debates during his long service in the Senate, Mr. Humphrey during the past four years has been directly involved, as a member of the National Security Council, in the decisions that led to deployment of the Sentinel system and apparent reversal of long-standing policy against anti-missile defense. In his 1968 campaign as the Democratic candidate for the Presidency Mr. Humphrey attempted to raise the issue for public debate—repeating Secretary McNamara's warning of the danger of plunging past Sentinel into an all-out arms race, and taking his own stand squarely against the ABM. He drew no direct response from Mr. Nixon, whose general statements appeared to constitute an endorsement of prevailing Defense Department policy under a commitment to "restore our objective of clear-cut military superiority." Mr. Humphrey here renews his plea for a full public airing of the larger strategic issues that lie behind the ABM.

The Center for the Study of Democratic Institutions presents this publication as a part of its effort to clarify the basic issues of our time and widen the circles of discussion about them.

Santa Barbara
January, 1969

INTRODUCTION
The State of the Question
Hubert H. Humphrey

America's determination to find ways of stabilizing the nuclear arms race will be severely tested in the coming days. President Nixon will be faced with a series of decisions that will irrevocably affect the security of this nation and the peace of the world. The new Congress will review these decisions and a spirited exchange of opinion on Capitol Hill is guaranteed. We are, in short, on the verge of a great debate on nuclear arms control, a debate whose outcome could well determine the survival of this country, not to mention the life and death of millions of other persons around the globe.

Yet the American people are shamefully ill informed on these matters. Decisions of far-reaching significance can be accomplished with only the slightest involvement of the informed and politically aware public. In a representative democracy this is unhealthy under any circumstances. When the survival of the planet may be involved, the situation becomes intolerable. That is why this volume is so important. It seeks to bring to the American people the facts on the most critical question in nuclear arms control: Should the United States build an anti-ballistic-missile defense system?

As President Nixon takes office, he will find that the basic decisions on the strategic issues posed by the ABM, far from being settled by the Congressional authorization that lies on his desk for a thin screen, are yet to be made. He will receive, as we did in the Johnson Administration, directly conflicting testimony from his scientific advisers as to the capability of the proposed anti-missile defenses; and he will receive conflicting intelligence estimates as to the Russians' capability to penetrate our defenses or shield themselves against our nuclear missiles. He stands now at the point where he must modify or reverse the recommendation of his military advisers; rest with the admittedly inadequate thin ABM system for which the Army is already selecting sites; or make a commitment to a heavy system that will by common agreement usher in another fateful stage in the nuclear arms race with the Soviet Union.

Throughout the Presidential campaign I emphasized that the most important question facing the new President would be that of negotiating an agreement with the Soviet Union to limit the strategic-arms competition. Despite the brutal invasion of Czechoslovakia by the Soviet Union and its dire consequences for East-West relations, both the United States and the Soviet Union continue to have a mutual interest in reaching such an agreement. The discussion over the ABM should be viewed in relation to this broader issue; the ABM issue is, however, the most immediate and potentially dangerous issue on the arms-control agenda. Although the ABM issue was not discussed in detail in the Presidential campaign, I have always been skeptical in my own mind about the security value of deploying an ABM system. I share the reservations stated by Secretary McNamara when he announced the ABM deployment in 1967. At the same time, I understood the reasons why the President felt that preparations for a limited deployment might quicken the interest of the Soviet Union in meaningful negotiations on the strategic-arms race, provided we place top priority on the urgent necessity of reaching an agreement on the ABM issue.

The ABM issue is not an easy one for the public to follow. It may be, as suggested by Dr. David R. Inglis of Argonne National Laboratory, that "The world's nuclear problems are too subtle for the average unconcerned citizen; the part most visible to him is the economic manna descending from the defense-industry haven." The trouble with that complacent view is that there is no longer any such thing as an unconcerned citizen, whether he knows it or not.

There are a good many reasons why the ABM controversy, which has raged within the government for almost a decade now, has been hard to follow. Official secrecy has had something to do with it, but not much. Although sometimes delayed and distorted by security regulations, the essential facts on such large strategic questions always come to light and find their way into general circulation. The description of the development of American ABM policy quoted from a paper published by the British Institute for Strategic Studies in the Preface to this volume is an example of the manner in which the information and estimates of the "intelligence community" are regularly publicized. Although a few details may be incorrect, or missing, the principal elements upon which the official policy-makers based their decisions are neatly laid out for all to see.

The record of the debate on *ABM: Yes or No?* that follows provides a valuable demonstration of how this kind of decision-making actually goes forward. As the reader will see, the participating scientists provide a hard core of factual analysis, usually reduced to numerical calculations suitable for a computer, and upon this base the strategists erect their structures of speculation and conjecture. It is, on the surface at least, comforting to come back to this solid collection of presumably measurable facts after a chilling exercise in what, in the nuclear era, has come to be called "thinking the unthinkable."

The very vocabulary of nuclear gamesmanship is uncomfortable for all but the most hardened practitioners. Neil

Jacoby notes that what economists ordinarily call "cost-benefit" analysis is changed to "cost-effectiveness" analysis in Pentagon parlance, "probably because it puts language under serious strain to refer to the death of a hundred million Russians or the destruction of a hundred billion dollars of Soviet capital as a benefit."

But one begins to suspect that this resort to the "facts" is not, as it appears, a return to reality but a retreat from it. Changing the vocabulary does not disguise the fact that the counters in the game are human lives, and the stake the fate of nations. Jerome Wiesner, who played it for years, calls it "the numbers game" and insists that it runs out of substance at the point at which it requires human judgment—as it always does.

Trying to explain to President Kennedy why scientists, who are supposed to be the most rational of people, could differ so on a technical issue, Wiesner pointed out that it is nature that is rational, not the scientists who try to explain natural processes:

Different people make different assumptions about all these elements. That is what is involved in the argument about anti-ballistic-missile systems. One man's assumptions give one set of conclusions; another man's assumptions give a different set. Some of the assumptions are essentially undefinable—we are talking about things we do not and cannot know anything about, no matter how we try. And so you can take whichever set of assumptions you choose.

Yet much of our most critical defense policy is being made on the basis of these numbers. And even so experienced a Washington hand as Dr. Jacoby, turning a skeptical economist's eye on the decision to put five billion dollars in the thin Sentinel ABM system, sets forth the cost analysis considerations involved and accepts the result because "presumably the Pentagon has plugged figures into the equations, run the calculations, and reached an affirmative conclusion."

We are living in an environment significantly affected by what President Eisenhower called the military-industrial complex and its principal offspring, the mammoth research and development budgets that sustain the defense establishment in the nuclear and missile age. R&D is a catalyst; by its nature it leads to far greater investments in the production of the goods and systems it makes possible. Thus every dollar spent on R&D has produced an expenditure of at least five dollars in military procurement alone. This diversion of funds into the military-industrial complex is widely recognized. What often escapes notice is the massive diversion of brainpower away from the civilian economy into the defense establishment. There inevitably arises among many of the individuals involved a disposition to justify defense expenditures, rather than to think in terms of national limitations on the production and dissemination of arms.

The principal points at issue in the ABM controversy are ably set forth in the following discussion. Here, as in the inner circles in Washington, they are advanced by men of great intellectual capacity and high moral purpose. In summary they are:

Challenge: The heavy ABM system will be the most complex technological system ever built by man, and there is no way to test it except under actual enemy attack. The odds are for at least a partial failure, and in this contest even a low percentage of missile penetration can be fatal.

Response: The military-industrial complex can meet the challenge and produce a system with a tolerable margin for error.

Challenge: Today's offensive missiles, with their improved penetration aids, probably could overcome the ABM system as now visualized, and the offensive improvement that its deployment is bound to stimulate certainly will render the system obsolete before it can be made operational.

Response: Any projected margin of failure for the defense system is not necessarily any greater than that for the offense.

Challenge: The cost is disproportionate to the protection ABM can afford.

Response: Potential deaths in an undefended United States are 120,000,000; ABM could reduce that casualty list to

40,000,000; the saving of 80,000,000 lives is not only a compelling humane consideration but involves our survival as a nation.

Challenge: ABM will intensify rather than restrain the arms race, worsening instead of improving U.S.-Soviet relationships.

Response: This does not necessarily follow. If the United States deploys an effective ABM system, the Russians might also shift their emphasis to defense, thus permitting a mutual de-escalation of the offensive missile race.

There is not, as Dr. Wiesner points out, any final proof here, only untested assumptions—and a man may come down in good conscience on either side, depending upon which set of assumptions he chooses. In closely following the development of missile policy over the years, I have myself found the most persuasive scientific argument on the side of restraint. I did not change that view when Secretary McNamara reluctantly compromised in favor of the thin ABM; it seemed to me that even in announcing it he made a better case against the new system than he did for it.

There is a grave omission in all this. The missile game is played almost entirely within the limits of scientific and military concepts; political considerations are largely dismissed as imponderables, relegated in the computer computations to a place along with such diversionary factors as the possibility of human error. The result is to predetermine the character of the game's result; the policy it produces is bound to be shaped within the limits of the military factors upon which it is predicated. We may have more missiles, or fewer, or missiles of a different type, but this is no more than addition and subtraction of the hardware of deterrence—and experience on both sides has indicated that the exercise leads inexorably to multiplication.

The tendency is to dismiss the political alternative to the balance of terror as entirely too risky—or at best to give it lip service. Well, politics is a risky business. But I would ask in all seriousness if it is any more difficult for the skilled and dedicated men who practice diplomacy to compute the odds on possible failure of a U.S.-Soviet disarmament treaty than it is for the scientists and strategists to determine the malfunctioning potential of the ABM. I do not believe it is; and if the question is to be decided by the simple assessment of risk, it ought to be pointed out that a diplomatic debacle would not necessarily be terminal, while an ABM failure certainly would be.

The truth is that we have been demanding more certain guarantees of success of those who have urged the positive course of negotiated disarmament than we have of those who insist that prudence requires us to rely on the negative protection of nuclear deterrence. The only proof of effectiveness that can be offered in defense of the missile standoff is that we have survived twenty years of international tensions without precipitating World War III.

The ABM is described by its proponents as defensive; but if it does achieve an effective missile screen, it could become offensive, since it would release strategic policy-makers from the restraints imposed by enemy second-strike capacity. The Russians will certainly recognize such an offensive potential, as we did when a rudimentary missile-defense system was deployed around Moscow several years ago.

It is contended that we can build up our defensive screen and our deterrent forces at the same time we actively pursue the goal of arms control and disarmament; indeed, it is argued that this is the only practical way we can proceed, since our adversaries will not respond to anything less than the clear threat of being outdistanced in the arms race. The history of the last decade seems to me to provide a monument to the fallacy of this theory.

So it is in the larger arena where we coexist uneasily with the Soviet Union, while sharing with the Russians the overt hostility of the People's Republic of China. I would be the first to agree with the dictum that the United States must negotiate with the communist world from a position of strength. But there is reason to doubt that we can any longer equate strength with military power alone. Secretary Clark Clifford, in his final report to the Congress, echoed the thoughts of his predecessor in the Defense Department by stressing that true national security is a compound of more than nuclear warheads and missiles. Another round in the nuclear arms race could only increase our *in*security, whereas achieving verifiable agreement with the Soviet Union to limit strategic offensive and defensive forces would enhance our security.

For a while, when the leaders of all the nations accepted the balance of terror as an inescapable fact of strategic life, we began to see our differences more clearly and to consider means by which they might be resolved without the use of the military force now denied the great powers, at least on a global scale. We did not resolve our ideological differences, nor reduce all our conflicts of interest; but as Justice Douglas notes in the concluding essay in this volume, we did achieve a substantial number of agreements and arrangements under which a great deal of useful international business has been conducted. We can draw at least a minimal lesson from that experience: We are not strangers any longer, and it is not ordained that we must again become enemies.

Robert McNamara, who has been as close to these matters as any man alive, ended his long tour in the Defense Department convinced that the most dangerous thing in the world is a state of mind—the belief among powerful men on both sides, in the face of all the horrendous evidence to the contrary, that somehow the scientists will yet find a way to employ nuclear weapons so that military men may again win a war. This is the real issue in the ABM controversy: When nations begin to accept the thesis that they may be able to devise adequate protection against nuclear attack, they also raise the possibility that they may yet be able to use decisively offensive missile force; and on the basis of a mixture of unfounded hopes and challenged assumptions they may turn away from serious negotiation and the effort to find a way to base international relations on liberating reason rather than paralyzing fear.

I say the time has come when we should take some risks in the name of peace rather than continue the great nuclear gamble in the name of security. In this light, the ABM might yet provide a great service in advancing the strategic-arms negotiations, if having taken the system to this stage of development, we set it aside as a symbol of our determination to halt the arms race where it is and turn it back if we can. Let us couple this with passage of the nuclear nonproliferation treaty now pending in the Senate, and go back to the negotiating table with the Russians. The application of as much energy, imagination, and determination in an honest effort to find a formula for arms control as we have invested in the effort to ring our cities with the ABM will, I am confident, bring greater rewards with less risk.

Many wise and experienced men in Washington who agree that this is what we should do insist that it cannot be done— that it is a political impossibility to reverse the policies that have produced, and are now shaped by, the military-industrial complex. It will be difficult, yes, but it is not impossible. For we cannot forget that our only chance of obtaining the huge volume of funds and talent required to rebuild American society at home lies in placing some limitation on the arms spiral. If we fail to do this, urgent domestic needs will go unmet.

What is needed now is a great expansion of the dialogue set forth in this volume: Let us get the issues out in the open, and get them clear. The fundamentals of the missile controversy are not beyond the comprehension of the American people, and certainly no decision of the magnitude of the ABM should be taken on their behalf without greater evidence of their informed consent than can be said to presently exist.

Waverly, Minnesota
January, 1969

The Case Against the ABM

Jerome B. Wiesner

"Can we continue to play this numbers game, which certainly will not buy a real defense, and at the same time achieve a rational world? My answer is no."

Dr. Karl Compton's sister, when living in India, watched a handyman driving a nail in a wall of her house, tearing up a lot of plaster in the process. In desperation she finally grabbed the hammer and nail and said: "My God, man, let me do that. Why don't you use some common sense?" He drew himself up in all his dignity and said: "Madam, common sense is a gift of God. I've only got a technical education."

What I have found hardest to learn in twenty years of dealing with military technology and international security problems is how to add a measure of common sense to them. Many other people have this problem, too. The whole issue of the ABM, I believe, ends up as a conflict of judgment rather than one of analysis. Making the analysis is very important because it provides the raw material for judgment; it gives some feeling for what is possible and what isn't. But very often it turns out that analyzing a complex situation offends plain

3

common sense or defies understanding. In studying a complex problem like the ABM, certain assumptions have to be made, and if the assumptions are bad, the analysis will simply conceal them.

This happens frequently and is happening now in the debates about the anti-ballistic missile. We do not have adequate knowledge about many aspects of an anti-ballistic-missile duel because we lack vital data about the attacking missiles and about ABM performance. So we just pick some numbers that seem rational, and we use them to make whatever point serves our purpose.

I once had an argument with James Webb and his staff about the best way to go to the moon. My calculations showed that the lunar orbit approach was much less certain than the earth orbit estimates on which his reliability values for each operation were based—a prime example was the reliability of starting an engine. When he became convinced his conclusion was suspect, Mr. Webb set his analysts to work and they came back with some new figures that proved their point. Now, it was hard for me to judge whether the restart probability of an engine that had never been built was going to be .9997 or .9998. And it was numbers of this kind, pyramided by the computer-full, that made the difference.

President Kennedy once said to me: "I don't understand. Scientists are supposed to be rational people. How can there be such differences on a technical issue?" I explained that it was nature that is rational, not the scientists, and that after scientists understand something, they can explain nature rationally; when they attempt to evaluate something that has not been built, they have to make assumptions about what can be done, how fast it can be done, how well it is going to work, and what its effectiveness will be. Different people make different assumptions about all these elements. That is what is involved in the argument about anti-ballistic-missile systems. One man's assumptions give one set of conclusions; another man's assumptions give a different set. Some of the assumptions are essentially undefinable—we are talking about things we do not and cannot know anything about, no matter how we try. And so you can take whichever set of assumptions you choose.

Of course, it gets even worse than that. When we design a system like the Sentinel and then analyze it, we assume almost idealized conditions. We assume it is going to work as specified, or we quite arbitrarily use some reliability estimate like .95. But we can't know whether that is even close to correct, because we have never built or operated anything like the Sentinel before. Even though the Sentinel is a very simple system (compared to the one that some people would really like to build once they get the Sentinel under the tent), it is probably the most complicated electronic system anyone has ever tried to put together. Here it is, the most elaborate, sophisticated, dynamic combination of rocketry, radars, computers, electronics, and other technology ever proposed, and we are expecting that it will work and work well, and not just well but perfectly the first time it is tried in a large-scale test. All kinds of mock tests can be invented for it, but the first genuine one will be when it is used in earnest. This contrasts with many weapons of the kind that were used in World War II, or now in Vietnam, where the soldiers must keep using them in spite of their defects until the military man understands their flaws and weaknesses and works his way around them or, if they are too defective, complains to the manufacturer and demands that they be straightened out. I would like to see the complaint the military writes to the manufacturer of the Sentinel system after it discovers that the computer program for discriminating "garbage" and incoming nuclear warheads was written wrong, like the computer in the last election that reported that 180 per cent of the population of a particular town had voted.

In my opinion any ABM is untestable. I am offering you this as a judgment, not a technical fact. But I think it is something that ought to be kept in mind by anyone who is trying to understand the more detailed technical arguments.

To judge an ABM defense system we must know its purpose. Is it supposed to provide an area defense, or defense of missile sites, or defense of a fleet, or defense of a few cities? It has to have some specific purpose, but one of the interesting things about the argument for the ABM is that its purpose seems very hard to grasp. We were told at one point that the Sentinel system was intended to protect us against irrational behavior on the part of the Chinese, though many people would contend that our existing deterrent system will do this adequately now. A careful analysis of the Sentinel system, however, does not show that Sentinel would provide protection against Chinese nuclear weapons for very long unless we make some unbelievably naive assumptions about the Chinese—that they do not have access to our journals and newspapers, for example, or that they are simply not thinking people.

I don't think we should spend much time talking about the Sentinel. We ought to regard the Sentinel as a bad joke perpetrated on us by Mr. McNamara and Mr. Johnson in an election year. It seems to me that their very rationalization—that it was to defend us against the Chinese, but we would stop building it if the Russians agreed not to build one—demonstrates that well enough.

We should look at the more general question of large anti-ballistic-missile systems and concentrate on what the military and the Congressional enthusiasts for the ABM would like to build, if they could get us to agree. What they have in mind is a much more sophisticated and elaborate anti-ballistic-missile system that would have the capability of intercepting missiles fired at the United States. The question is: Does it make all that much difference to our security if an ABM system can shoot down some fraction of the ballistic missiles aimed at our cities? What, in fact, is the general, over-all effect on our security of creating an ABM system? How does it change our deterrent posture? How much protection, if any, will it give the country at large or the military installations? What is its effect on our efforts to achieve a more rational world? What does it do to a variety of other military objectives we might have?

Before we approach such questions, there is one important generalization I would like to stress, one that should always be kept in mind while examining strategic-weapons systems but that people almost always forget to take into account. It is that these developments take a long time from conception to effective operational deployment. This gives a kind of inherent stability to the character of the military-technical race. To appreciate this fact, we need only to think back to some of the frights that did not materialize—the missile gap and the bomber gap, for example. It takes time and effort to change the strategic balance drastically. The development from the research stage, which itself takes time, to the prototype stage takes even more time, as do the testing and debugging of anything so complicated. Engineering it into a produceable device takes more time, its production takes time, its deployment into the field takes time. Finally it is operational, and then, if it is a defensive weapon, it is generally also obsolete. This whole cycle takes about ten years.

Some weapons systems are obsolete in their conception, and I think this is probably true for the anti-ballistic-missile system we have before us. I have, in fact, come to the conclusion that any system that depends on projectiles—rather than, say, on nuclear rays or electromagnetic beams or laser beams—is futile.

In 1961, when President Kennedy first began to survey his military problems, his attention was drawn forcefully to an anti-missile system, the Nike-Zeus. He began to get a flood of mail, from friends, from Congress, from people in industry. The press pointedly questioned him about his plans to deploy the Nike-Zeus system. He began to see full pages for it in popular magazines like *Life* and *Saturday Evening Post*, proclaiming how Nike-Zeus would defend America and listing the industrial towns that would profit from the contracts for it—advertisements, by the way, that were generally paid for with government money as contract expenses. (The law no longer permits such advertising to be charged to contracts.) This pressure built up to the point where President Kennedy came to feel that the only thing anybody in the country was concerned about was the Nike-Zeus. He began to collect Nike-Zeus material. In one corner of a room he had a pile of literature and letters and other materials on the subject. He set out to make himself an expert on the Nike-Zeus and spent hundreds of hours gathering views from the scientific community about it. In the end he decided not to deploy Nike-Zeus. Then something interesting happened. As soon as the decision was made against Nike-Zeus, everybody admitted that it was no good. People began to point out weaknesses in the system—that, for example, it was a system with very little discrimination between what it ought to intercept and the decoys fired to confuse it. Even Mr. McNamara said that to have deployed the Nike-Zeus would have been a very serious mistake.

An anti-ballistic-missile system attempts to intercept and destroy ballistic missiles coming in very fast, very high, from long distances. It requires that the defenders fire their own intercepting missiles from the ground after they have detected the incoming missiles with a long-range radar. Detection normally occurs when the attacking missiles are several hundred miles away if their trajectories are normal. They can be detected farther away if forward radars are employed. After detection one makes a rough projection or prediction of the trajectory of the incoming missile and launches an anti-missile, usually a rocket carrying a nuclear warhead, in the direction of the incoming device. The missile-tracking radar on the ground must follow the incoming warhead and tell the anti-missile rocket where to go. When the defensive rocket gets close enough to the incoming missile, its nuclear warhead is exploded and, in principle, destroys the attacking object. This has been demonstrated both by analysis and in field tests to be possible. No one questions that if you set up this kind of system, it will work in an ideal situation.

However, there were several things wrong about the Nike-Zeus that would have made it relatively ineffective in real situations. First, as originally designed, it was supposed to intercept incoming missiles at very high altitudes, out of the atmosphere. This meant that it was easily confused; an enemy could mix real nuclear missiles with lightweight decoys made to look like missiles and send them in against Nike-Zeus, so that it would be totally saturated. To correct this we allowed the incoming devices to come down into the atmosphere; the differ-ence in weights allowed the heavy pieces, the real warheads, to go on, while all this other lightweight decoy junk was slowed down and separated out. This tended to work somewhat better, but even so, the whole system as conceived really wasn't good enough. It could not respond fast enough. Its radars weren't good enough. Its traffic-handling capacity—that is, the number of missiles it could deal with at one time—was not adequate.

Also, Nike-Zeus was subject, as I believe all the later systems are, to something called blackout; that is, if a nuclear explosion were set off to destroy an incoming missile, it also upset the gas in the air, "ionized" it—electrons strip off from the molecules, and for a while the gas acts like a metal rather than a gas so that radar waves cannot go through it and you cannot see what is behind it. Nike-Zeus was open to this in two ways. First, if you fired some rockets and they set off their own nuclear weapons, you might generate self-blackout. Second, if the enemy recognized that the defense had this vulnerability, he could design his offensive system to occasionally dump in a rocket with a nuclear warhead, explode it, and generate enough ionization to black out your radars. But, Nike-Zeus had another interesting weakness—by the time it had been brought down to a reasonably low altitude so that the atmosphere would filter incoming devices, no one could be sure that when it set off its nuclear explosion it would not damage itself.

Nike-Zeus was a point-defense system, and this posed two more problems. First, which points in the United States would be defended? This presented a terrible political problem. Would we defend the twenty-five largest cities? The fifty larg-est? Second, it was possible for an intelligent enemy to bypass the point-defense system and land his nuclear weapons in the countryside, just outside the range of the system, generating a fallout attack on the population. This required that if we were to deploy Nike-Zeus, we would have to build fallout shelters on a grand scale.

As I said, once Nike-Zeus was turned off, even its strongest proponents admitted it had fatal weaknesses, and they undertook to try to fix them. The worst weaknesses of Nike-Zeus have now been eliminated. The new system, Nike-X, of which the Sentinel uses some pieces—but which is certainly not what is being proposed as the full ABM to defend the United States— is improved in almost every respect. Its radars are electrically scanned; they can look in all directions very rapidly. The radars have higher power so they can see farther. The Sentinel has two intercept rockets, one designed for low altitude, called Sprint, that can get up there fast and maneuver quickly; another called Spartan, for long-range interception. It has a computer system better able to discriminate between trash and nuclear warheads in the incoming package.

We have also changed, at least in principle, the way in which we would destroy incoming nuclear warheads. Still another problem with the Nike-Zeus was that its destruction of the incoming nuclear weapons depended on a phenomenon called neutron heating. When one explodes a nuclear weapon near another nuclear weapon, a flux of neutrons is released; these penetrate into the guts of the second nuclear weapon and heat it enough to melt it. However, this effect does not work over very great distances; so the Nike-Zeus presented us with the problem that a single defensive nuclear explosion could be effective against only a limited number of incoming targets. Although I do not think that cost factors are the most important part of the argument against the ABM, this did create an economic case against it.

Well, in Sentinel, at very high altitudes, we have gone over to another phenomenon called X-ray kill. We have substituted nuclear weapons that can generate an intense flux of X-rays, which are effective at greater distances than the neutrons. The difficulty with all of this is that it produces a kind of electronic Maginot Line. The defender sits and guesses about the attacker's tactics. If he guesses that one thing is going to happen, he invents a technology to deal with it. If he guesses that something else is going to happen, he invents another technology. But there is always the possibility that something quite unexpected will happen. I do not think the defender is ever going to know really what to expect; the variety of techniques available to a nation planning an offensive system is great enough to keep an anti-ballistic-missile system of the kind we are talking about totally off balance.

As a matter of fact, just the thought that we might develop an anti-ballistic-missile system, and therefore that the Russians might do the same thing, caused us to develop a whole set of offensive countermeasures that make our Air Force and Navy confident that we do not have to worry about a Russian anti-missile system. We have some new missiles that carry several warheads with high accuracy instead of a single one. We have available—and so do they—the possibility of using the blackout attack. One can develop very different kinds of offensive rockets that come in at low altitudes and do various elaborate maneuvers. We can shield against X-rays. The choices are endless.

So, as I said in the beginning, anyone who makes calculations about what his defense system can do must make and proceed from a series of assumptions that do not seem to be warranted. But, of course, this does not stop people from making the assumptions.

In his 1967 Defense Posture speech, for example, former Defense Secretary McNamara cited some figures still widely quoted. He said a nuclear exchange with Russia in 1967 would cause 120 million American deaths. He then postulated two anti-missile defense systems for the United States—one, Posture A, would cost $10 billion, and the other, Posture B, would cost $20 billion. His calculations indicated that the $10-billion system would reduce American fatalities to 40 million deaths, while the $20-billion system would reduce American fatalities to 30 million. These are numbers I find hard to grasp, but they obviously are meant to indicate a very substantial improvement in the fatality ratio if we were to build a defense system. However, more questions were left unanswered than were answered in the calculations. First, Mr. McNamara, I believe, assumed the system would work as planned. But, let me repeat,

I have serious reservations about the effectiveness of such an ABM system even if a potential enemy were not devising things to undo its effectiveness. I do not think its performance would be anywhere near the advertised predictions because of its very complexity. Second, Mr. McNamara said he had made his calculations on the basis of the 1967 Soviet offensive-missile deployment. But that was not a Soviet deployment the Russians told us about; it was McNamara's guess, or somebody's guess, about the Soviet deployment. So our defense planners must have had to make certain assumptions not only about our own system's weakness and accuracy but also about how fast the Russian missiles would come in, how well they would be protected, whether they would bear one warhead or two or more. Maybe Mr. McNamara knew all these things. But I suspect there were a lot of assumptions in his calculation that might not hold up. Even if they were made, I doubt that they would be of much use today.

Mr. McNamara said that the 1967 Soviet land-based missile force was 750 missiles, and he estimated their future growth on a basis of past experience. I doubt if anyone today questions that the Soviet force is at least one third larger than it was in 1967; it grew much faster than predicted. So even the simple estimate of the Soviet force was wrong. Furthermore, the United States could not have built the ABM system Mr. McNamara was talking about in the time available between 1967, when the calculation was made, and today. It would have taken five or six or seven years to build it. So Mr. McNamara would have to have had the nerve to guess what a Russian deployment would be in 1975 in order to have made a meaningful estimate for that time period. He obviously had sense enough not to try.

Unfortunately, many people do not read the fine print. They do not realize that you cannot snap your fingers and wish into existence the kind of an anti-ballistic-missile system being argued about. They do not realize that if we build an anti-ballistic-missile system and the Russians regard it as something they do not like, they have plenty of time to respond and to figure out how to get their missiles past it, or that if they build an ABM system, we have time to respond in the same way.

In essence, then, my judgment is that we are just as likely to wind up a captive in the arms race if we start going the way of ABM defense as if we continue to build more and more offensive missiles.

There are people who say that it is better to spend your money on ABM defenses than on more destructive power. If one could do this—that is, freeze the offensive power on both sides and build only defensive systems—this might make the ABM a good thing. If Congress, the military, and the manufacturers were happy to build only defenses and did not press us to add to the offensive forces, maybe the ABM would be a good buy.

But I do not believe that this is a tenable situation, and this is the reason for one basic disagreement on the ABM. I think we would reach a point in the growth of the ABM defensive system where people would argue that improved defenses mean that the offenses no longer can guarantee deterrence and that we must therefore increase our offensive capability even more.

This is not a matter that anybody can settle with numbers and calculations. It is a judgment. But judgments of this kind are at the heart of the decision to build or not to build an ABM system, not the statistics, the calculations about "cost effectiveness," or how many people will be killed. These factors are important in the decision, of course. What is most important, however, is the total dynamics and the likely interaction of the policy-makers on both sides. I come back to where I began and ask: Can we continue to play this numbers game, which certainly will not buy a real defense, and at the same time achieve a rational world? My answer is no.

And then I must add this last fillip to it: I believe that the situation will be made more, not less, dangerous. We always underestimate our own capabilities and overestimate those of the other fellow. I think this is true of both sides, and it generates what I call a parallax effect. That is, if the Russians build a defensive system, we think it is better than it is, so we overbuild in order to penetrate it, and vice versa. Thus there is the real possibility that when everything is stabilized at some higher level and we are all relaxed because we have become used to it, the potential for destruction will have gone up instead of down.

George S. McGovern

". . . it would be a national blunder of major proportions—militarily, politically, and diplomatically —for the United States to deploy a defensive missile system on the basis of our present knowledge about the ABM and about the international situation into which we propose to inject this dubious new armament system."

The anti-ballistic missile is a remarkable device. It is remarkable for its technology and for its capacity to devour rather large sums of money. But most remarkable of all is its political effect —an effect so potent that our country is about to embark on the deployment of this defensive missile system before it has been carefully evaluated and during the precise period in our national life when we ought to be most interested in reducing both the costs and the hazards of the arms race.

I have already recorded in the Senate my own conviction, at least my tentative conviction, that it would be a national blunder of major proportions—militarily, politically, and diplomatically—for the United States to deploy a defensive missile system on the basis of our present knowledge about the ABM and about the international situation into which we propose to inject this dubious new armament system.

I am convinced that the proposed ABM would be obsolete

before it could be constructed. I read the evidence to indicate that the Soviet Union could very quickly overwhelm such a system with considerably smaller investment in their offensive capability. This, after all, is precisely what we have done in recent years in response to the very limited ABM system we think is now being deployed around Moscow.

No one has more clearly summarized the case against a full-blown ABM system than did former Secretary of Defense Robert McNamara when he said on September 18, 1967:

Every ABM system that is now feasible involves firing defensive missiles at incoming offensive warheads in an effort to destroy them. But what many commentators on this issue overlook is that any such system can rather obviously be defeated by an enemy simply sending more offensive warheads, or dummy warheads, than there are defensive missiles capable of disposing of them. This is the whole crux of the nuclear action-reaction phenomenon.

Then Mr. McNamara added:

Were we to deploy a heavy ABM system throughout the United States [and keep in mind that it is the heavy system that is being discussed here, not the phony, so-called thin China-oriented Sentinel system] the Soviets would clearly be strongly motivated to so increase their offensive capability as to cancel out our defensive advantage. It is futile for each of us to spend $4 billion, or $40 billion, or $400 billion—and at the end of all the spending, at the end of all the deployment, and at the end of all the effort, to be relatively at the same point of balance on the security scale that we are now.

I believe that an ABM deployment by the United States would actually decrease our security and our capacity to conduct an intelligent and rational foreign policy. It would do this not only because it would be easily penetrated by the Soviet Union at less cost, if they chose to do so, but also because it would lead to a further escalation of the arms race and a worsening of Soviet-American relations.

Beyond these considerations, the allocation of many billions of dollars of public funds to the ABM at this time would weaken the nation by depriving us of funds urgently needed to cope with explosive social and economic needs of our own society and of the world in ferment around it.

We could, as a precaution, do what I assume we would do if we had the good judgment to back away from the actual *deployment* of this missile system—that is, continue with research and development, even to the prototype stage, on defensive missile systems. Then, if new breakthroughs should occur on the technical front or if new information comes to us about what our potential enemies are up to, we would be in a position, if necessary, to consider deployment of the system. This is the prudent alternative to plunging ahead now in the face of highly doubtful knowledge and present technical difficulties. And it is not only a sound, businesslike, and scientific approach to the matter; it also gives us diplomatic flexibility at a critical moment in our relationship with the Soviet Union. The possibility of an arms agreement between the Russians and ourselves that would make it possible for each side to scale down both defensive and offensive missile spending is considered a real prospect by almost all observers—if neither side tilts the balance.

When the Administration yielded to the pressure of the military and agreed to deploy a thin ABM system supposedly oriented toward China, this could not, in my judgment, be accepted as a security decision based on a broad view of national and international priorities. It was rather a surrender to mounting political pressure from military-minded Senators and Congressmen and generals and arms manufacturers and their supporters. And all of this was fed by the mistaken impression that it is possible and reasonable to calculate national security in mathematical terms related almost exclusively to the capacity of our defensive and offensive armaments.

As Dr. Wiesner has reminded us, the political heat on the President and on the Department of Defense to deploy the ABM did not suddenly appear in 1967. For more than a decade pressure had been directed in the most intensive fashion against President Eisenhower, later against President Kennedy, and throughout his Administration against President Johnson. All three Chief Executives—different as they were in political background and orientation—staunchly resisted the demands, first for Nike-Zeus, then for the Nike-X system. The important point is that if they had surrendered earlier, as President Johnson finally did, those systems would have been built and would now be totally obsolete and worthless to us. We would have only the waste of $30 billion or $35 billion for our efforts.

I am confident that the system now being proposed will prove equally obsolete and equally worthless by the time it can be deployed. I believe that when President Johnson finally bent before the ABM deployment pressure, he committed what may prove to be, next to the escalation of the war in Vietnam, the most costly blunder of his Administration. President-elect Nixon could perform an invaluable service to the American people and to the cause of peace if he would begin not only by ending our military involvement in Vietnam but also by reversing the ill-advised authorization of the ABM system. In doing so he would only be returning to the strategic concept that has served the world well in the postwar years—recognizing that the only real defense against the sophisticated missile system of the Soviet Union is our continued capacity to deter the use of that system, if in fact the Soviets ever seriously consider using it.

The Johnson Administration attempted to justify the abandonment of its own previous, clearly articulated opposition to the ABM by offering the system as a temporary $5-billion holding action against China's predicted nuclear capability by the early 1970's. This rationalization soon became so patently absurd, as information became available about the delay in China's missile development, that the argument was dropped before the debate even got underway on the Senate floor. I got no answer when I asked the proponents of the ABM why they had billed this new system as a defense against China and then declared a few weeks later that the system could be abandoned if the Russians would agree not to build one.

The truth is that if we begin deploying a $5-billion thin system, political and economic pressures will very quickly accelerate until we have poured $20 billion or $30 billion or $50 billion or perhaps a $100 billion into this system. I do not believe many members of Congress seriously doubt that this is the case. If the Nixon Administration chose to join with those of us who are fighting ABM, I am confident we could head off this explosive, destructive exercise in futility.

As you know, the Congress, and particularly the Senate, has been subjected to much information and argument on ABM—some of it behind closed doors for security reasons. This leaves the impression that the matter is hopelessly technical. It isn't really. Congressmen can understand what is at issue here and recognize that the real questions are primarily political in nature.

One point to be emphasized is that any system of defense against thermonuclear missiles is qualitatively different from the bomber defenses of World War II. In that war it was assumed by both attackers and defenders that on any given raid most of the bombers would reach their target, most would drop their bombs at least somewhere in the vicinity of the target and would damage it if they did not destroy it, and most would return to their bases to fly again on future missions. The job of the defender, then, was to impose such a heavy attrition on the attacking bombers that destruction of the target would not be worth the price in lost men and striking power. Generally this critical attrition rate was surprisingly low. For example, on that famous night during the Battle of Britain when the defenders were able to destroy just five per cent of the attacking German bomber force, the battle was won. The bombers did not return.

But missile warfare is as different as night from day. The smallest thermonuclear warhead is still considerably more powerful than the Hiroshima and Nagasaki bombs that ended the war against Japan. One warhead can destroy any significant target, except a few of our largest cities, which would require two or three warheads for total devastation. So, while a five-per-cent-effective air defense won the Battle of Britain twenty-five years ago, ten or even fifteen times that effectiveness would be meaningless in a thermonuclear war. Every significant target probably would be attacked by a dozen or more missiles averaging perhaps four or five warheads each, so that even a ninety-per-cent-effective missile defense could not prevent a catastrophe of unspeakable proportions in the defended country.

One should also keep in mind that the Soviet Union is not likely to remain static if we proceed in the deployment of an ABM system. The only reasonable assumption is that the Soviets would respond the same way we did when we began to get evidence that they were deploying a limited defense system around one city, Moscow. For a relatively modest expenditure we began to develop the kind of penetration aids and multiple warheads that have already enabled us to overwhelm that system. And, of course, this has left the Soviets in a much more vulnerable position in the event of a nuclear exchange than they were in before they began deploying their anti-ballistic-missile system.

The history of this kind of escalatory defense-offense spiral demonstrates that the defense always labors under at least two very serious disadvantages. The first is mathematical. Let us take a hypothetical situation. Currently the Soviets have approximately one thousand offensive warheads. If we were to build a ninety-per-cent-effective ABM defense system, we must assume that they still would be capable of reaching us with a hundred warheads—and loss of American lives would still be calculated in tens of millions.

Now suppose the Soviets recognized the survival value of our ninety-per-cent-effective ABM system by increasing their warheads from the present 1,000 to 4,000 or 5,000 (which is what we did, in effect, with the conversion of our Polaris missiles to the Poseidon system and the addition of multiple warheads to our Minutemen). Our ABM screen then would let through not 100 warheads, but 400 or 500. If we wanted to maintain the pre-ABM Soviet response level of "only" 100 hits on our country, we would have to build an ABM system so tight it could knock down ninety-eight per cent of 4,000 to 5,000 incoming warheads.

No one in his wildest fancy has ever suggested that a ninety-eight-per-cent-effective missile defense is a technical possibility. In fact, the probability is that during a heavy attack the effectiveness of the ABM system would drop to near zero, since thermonuclear explosions set off in the atmosphere create their own radar blackout.

The ABM's second inherent disadvantage is economic. Some have said that if it could be demonstrated that it would cost a hundred times as much to deploy an ABM system as it would to make the offensive missiles to overcome it, they would not advocate it. Well, I don't know whether it would cost a hundred times as much or not. But I do know that we are converting our Polaris missiles to the Poseidon system, which enormously increases their striking power, for a cost of about $3.2 billion. And I do know that the $5-billion Sentinel system we are talking about as a defensive system would be rendered totally useless by a $3-billion investment similar to the one we made in our offensive power in the Poseidon system. Poseidon would go through Sentinel like a hot knife through butter. The heavy ABM system is projected at a minimum cost of $20 billion, and even that would be no match for the offensive Poseidon-type system we brought in for $3 billion. Those ratios may not be sufficient to get advocates of an ABM system over to my side, but they are certainly not insignificant.

Given the high levels of offensive armament that both the major powers will have by the mid-1970's, the proposed terminal ABM system, even in its heaviest form, would from all indications that I have seen be ineffective. And this is a system that could easily cost a $100 billion if one includes the cost of the fallout shelters that many experts believe will be necessitated by the Sprint anti-ballistic missile now included as a part of the full system.

Why, then, are the Joint Chiefs of Staff recommending that such vast sums be spent, and why has a majority of the Congress already approved this decision? Curiously, the debate over construction seems almost irrelevant to the actual decision-making process. I have been actively involved in the debate on the ABM from the very beginning. I was much impressed when Senator Stuart Symington, the former Secretary of the Air Force who at one time was considered sympathetic to the ABM, explained in great detail why he now believes the system is militarily ineffective and would represent an enormous waste of public funds. This, by any definition, was informed, expert testimony, and I have waited for an effective rebuttal by the ABM proponents. It has never come.

Neither have we had from the scientific community any really convincing arguments as to the effectiveness of this system. You will note the heavy qualifications that mark the pro-ABM arguments in this discussion. I think the reason for this is that the military and scientific arguments against the ABM do not need to be rebutted because the compulsion for funding the ABM is not really military and scientific at all—but economic and political.

Politically, the ability to get support for highly dubious multi-billion-dollar projects such as the ABM rests on two factors: first, exploitation of the national feeling of insecurity that comes any time we debate a proposal with a defense label attached to it; and second, the perfectly legal and very substantial rewards the military sector can bestow upon communities and states whose Congressmen are co-operative.

I am not implying that supporters of the ABM have sold their souls to the armament lobby. These men, many of whom are among the most respected of my colleagues, are acting in what they believe is the interest of their constituents. The creation, the continuance, or the abolition of defense plants or installations affects the jobs and the lives of thousands of people. Supporters of projects like these seek through a kind of process of rationalization to serve their constituents' interest. So, let us face it, the anti-ballistic-missile system is little more than a gigantic make-work welfare project sponsored by the military-industrial complex. I charge that this kind of artificial and unimaginative public spending degrades rather than strengthens our society, and that it does so to an extent that more than offsets the highly questionable military advantages.

What is needed is a prudent and imaginative foreign policy that will guarantee our national interests by other than primarily military means. Such a policy would open the way to rational limits of arms production. We also need to take steps to meet the economic fears of beleaguered Congressmen and defense-oriented communities by means some of us suggested in the Congress five years ago: that is, an economic conversion act to assist our defense industries and local communities by converting excessive military capacity to the production of urgently needed civilian facilities.

We live in a great and affluent country. But it is a country now confronted by the most urgent domestic needs. It is not too much to say that an even greater threat to our survival than any posed by nuclear missiles may lie in our present inability to redirect the floodtide of money and resources flowing into the military sectors toward rebuilding and reconstructing a great society.

What is at stake is the quality of our country, which can be restored and maintained only by a wiser utilization of our resources and more meaningful expression of the human spirit.

The Case for the ABM

Donald G. Brennan

"The ABM is not intended to kill anything but lethal offensive missiles. It is intended to preserve human lives. . . . We can, if we work at it intelligently, have both sound defenses and a world free of the apprehensions and waste of a major arms race."

On the whole I accept Jerome Wiesner's technical characterizations. I think he put his finger on some of the sources of the scientific disagreements over the ABM defensive system.

I accept, more or less, his characterization of the Sentinel system as it was originally envisaged. The views I present here are in support of a defense that would make a substantial difference against a Soviet missile attack, a system of a character and capacity missing in the original conception of Sentinel.

Here is what I deem to be the critical factor: Most of the studies of performance of heavier deployment of ABM defenses now possible against major Soviet attacks—assuming that the Soviets do not make a major increase in their offensive forces in response to our improved defense—have shown that fatalities in the United States might be reduced from something in the range of 80 to 100 to 120 million down to perhaps 20 or 30 or 40 million. Using the period of the mid-1970's as a statistical base,

27

such a reduction would change the fatality level from something like half the population to something on the order of ten per cent. Obviously, the remaining prospect of losing ten per cent of our citizens is hardly likely to make one enthusiastic. But these calculations could make a very great difference in the kind of United States that would exist after an act of nuclear war.

By the same process that might save as much as ninety per cent of the populace, we would very likely be saving an even higher percentage of the country's productive capacity, communications, and transportation system. This makes a very great difference in the ability of the society to recover from such a blow—a degree of difference that other types of defense, notably traditional civil defense, cannot make, so far as we can foresee. So the first observation I offer is that if the ABM defense systems perform more or less as expected, they can make an enormous difference in the future of the country following an exchange of nuclear weapons.

I concede that the ABM systems are large, complicated, and untested in any final sense. There is some chance that if subjected to the ultimate test of war, they may fail in ways that we did not foresee. This is a technical problem, as Dr. Wiesner says, and any scientist must agree it exists. But there is another side of this technical interaction that he did not mention and I would emphasize; that is, the offensive forces that may be fired against this defensive system also are large, complicated, untested systems—untested against the environment in which they are supposed to work.

Scientists in the current state of the art may have more confidence that a given offensive missile will reach its target than that a defensive system will head it off. But of course it can happen that the offense, too, may contain weaknesses not discovered in advance of its actual employment. The defense may perform worse than predicted, but it also may perform very much better than design-center expectations. There really are two sides to this coin. And if we are talking about the possibility of buying national survival insurance, some degree of risk that the insurance wouldn't pay off under some circumstances does not necessarily negate its insurance value.

This brings us to the technical question of how difficult it is for the offense to nullify an ABM defense. The war-outcome estimates made by Secretary McNamara should obtain if the Soviets do not work very hard at nullifying our defense. If they work very hard at counteracting our ABM system, they conceivably could cancel the insurance value we expected to purchase with the new defenses—unless, of course, their offense failed altogether, which we are certainly not likely to be counting on.

Well, it turns out that, so far as we can see, it is indeed hard for them to shift the balance by further offensive development. This is a point I wish to stress. One of the considerations that killed Nike-Zeus (and I was among those who were opposed to deploying it) was that the system looked easy to nullify. It had these mechanically slewed radars; it did not have much tracking capability. The conclusion was that it would be fairly easy to design attack systems that would penetrate it.

However, the best kinds of defenses that have been developed in the last several years do not suffer from those deficiencies. While I agree with Dr. Wiesner that economic factors do not dominate here, one wants to have some sense of the costs.

If the Soviets could nullify one of these $10-billion or $20-billion ABM defense systems by spending only an additional one per cent as much on their offensive force, then I, among many others, would agree that the ABM is a very bad buy. It seems, however, not likely to be any such minor economic matter. In order to wholly nullify one of the major ABM defenses now under consideration the Soviets would have to spend as much or possibly even more money on their offensive forces as we would have spent on the defense in the first place.

There were many authoritative statements made in the past to the effect that it is relatively inexpensive to improve an offensive system to nullify an ABM defense, but this fact has not been true since 1964–1965. So far as one can see from detailed current studies, offensive and defensive cost factors have been balanced out, at least, for the past four years or more.

How stable are the estimates of performance I am citing here? Specifically, those are the claims that without an adequate ABM system we might lose, say, half the populace in a Soviet nuclear attack, while a substantial defense might save eighty to ninety per cent of the total populace and a proportionate share of production and communications capacity; and that it is not cheap or easy for the potential enemy to nullify the system that would make this possible.

This is the kind of question one cannot answer with guarantees. We must concede all the uncertainties Dr. Wiesner cites. It may be useful to try to put the issue in perspective with a comparison. We have come to have a lot of confidence in the security of the Polaris-submarine component of the United States deterrent force. What is the source of this confidence? It comes from the fact that we have spent a half billion dollars a year on research and development trying to find cheap and reliable ways of killing Polaris submarines, and nobody has found them. We can find cheap and unreliable ways of killing them, and we can find expensive and reliable ways of killing them. But the combination of cheap and reliable ways has not been found despite the best efforts of a lot of good people who have spent a lot of time looking. It is basically because of this negative fact that we tend to consider the Polaris a pretty good part of our deterrent force.

Well, it is beginning to be true—it isn't as yet completely true, I agree, but it is beginning to be true—that a like statement can be made on behalf of missile defenses as against the possibility of penetrating these defenses. We have spent about a half billion dollars a year for four or five years (since the prospects of strong defenses have come into serious technical view) on means of penetrating these defenses. But nobody has yet found a cheap and reliable way of penetrating a good ABM defense—although, of course, this is not an argument that a cheap and reliable penetration technique cannot be found.

Of course, I have to concede that we are comparing two quite different situations. In the Polaris submarine case, we are talking about vessels that may escape altogether so far as detection and destruction is concerned. In the missile-defense case we are not talking about the defending country escaping scot-free. Nobody studying missile defenses believes that one can even begin to count on an absolutely impervious shield. I am talking only about the probability of holding fatalities to the range of ten to twenty per cent.

Now, in terms of the insurance value of reducing fatalities to that level, it is beginning to appear that these estimates have the kind of stability that we have come to associate with the invulnerability of Polaris submarines. It can still happen that next week somebody will find a device or perfect an invention that will cancel or seriously alter every figure I have used here. But there are beginning to be very good grounds for being skeptical that any such thing is likely to happen.

I would offer a more technical argument on behalf of the future prospect of defenses. While, as Dr. Wiesner said, there are many ways one can think of to penetrate a defense, there also are more and more varied ways one can think of to build up a defense. I believe that essentially all the possible means of penetration are more or less known and openly discussed. We can make warheads that maneuver. They can come in at low angles. They can come in at high angles. They can come in on special trajectories. We can put in more warheads, more chaff, more decoys, more jammers. But with it all, there is a fairly small spectrum of things of this kind that can be tried with an offense to make it work better, at least for several years.

To my mind, there is a much larger array of possibilities of a technical sort in which one might place hope that the defense can be made to work better. Dr. Wiesner alluded to some of these in passing, such as lasers and orbiting systems of non-nuclear interceptors. There is a much larger catalogue of very diverse developments that have at least some likelihood of contributing to a major breakthrough on the defensive side.

Agreeing that these technical estimates cannot be exact, I believe they are nevertheless very important in establishing ranges for decision-making. For example, if I were convinced that improved ABM defenses could be neutralized for a minor fraction of their cost, or that they would only make a ten per cent difference in the fatality levels in case of nuclear attack, I would stop being interested in defense myself. As it is, the technical estimates seem to me to make a case that cannot be ignored.

Dr. Wiesner refers to his concern that if the Soviets begin building up a heavy defense, our military strategists would be apprehensive about the ability of our offense to penetrate it; this, therefore, would soon upset any understanding about stabilization of offensive forces on both sides and would launch a new arms race.

I do not myself believe, and I am sure Dr. Wiesner does not believe, that the United States requires as a fundamental part of its national security some fixed destruction capability—the capacity to destroy, say, seventy-four million Russians, or seventy-six per cent of Soviet industrial capacity, to cite two numbers Mr. McNamara has used in his discussion of requirements for what he calls an assured destruction capacity for our deterrent force.

As a matter of fact, I do not believe that the United States has any fixed requirement for any large number of Soviet hostages. It seems to me that our basic military requirement is simply to make sure that we are not in a bad position vis-à-vis the Soviets at any given or predictable time. If we are confident that we are in a fair military position vis-à-vis the Soviets, there is no fundamental law of nature requiring that we should be able to destroy seventy-four million Russians. In 1936, to pick a date at random, we knew we couldn't kill seventy-four million Russians or any perceptible fraction thereof, and nobody here was very upset about it. I think that we could begin to work backward toward a state of that kind, in which defenses begin to look more and more effective—and, as far as I am concerned, I am perfectly willing that defenses should look effective on both sides.

Dr. Wiesner's view—and he has pointed to this as our basic difference here—is that neither our country nor the Soviet

Union would accept a move in that direction. This view seems to accept the idea that for the indefinite future effective offenses will be based on a fixed requirement that we be able to kill, if not seventy-four million Russians, then twenty million Russians, or whatever number. I do not think that is the case, and I do not believe the senior members of the military staffs think it is the case. I know many high-ranking officers—including, if I am not mistaken, General Leon Johnson—who do not accept any fixed requirement for the destruction of a large number of Soviet hostages, so long as we are in a relatively favorable defensive position ourselves.

I might remark on how the offensive-deterrent theory came to have the kind of pervasiveness it has enjoyed in the past several years. The technical prospects for defense in the later 1950's were rightly judged to be poor. As a result many of us assimilated the doctrine that since the United States and the Soviet Union could not effectively defend against each other, each had to deter the other with large nuclear capability. There was no really good alternative. Today, when the beginnings of an alternative are emerging, we seem to be seeing the emergence of a distorted form of this doctrine of deterrence, namely, that since we must deter, we cannot defend. That, I suggest, is a *non-sequitur*.

I should like to discuss another common argument against ballistic-missile defenses, although Dr. Wiesner did not mention it. This is the theory that anything that makes war more tolerable makes it more likely. But "more tolerable" in this instance means 20 or 30 million American people killed instead of a 120 million; the lesser prospect is hardly likely to lead to dancing in the streets. I suggest that under the minimum foreseeable circumstances nobody is going to get button-happy. It is very unlikely that you could find any American decision-maker whose behavior in a crisis, so far as his propensity for starting a nuclear war is concerned, is going to be significantly altered because he is told that his action will cost the lives of "only 30 million," instead of, say, 100 million. And my reading of the Soviet bureaucracy, which is very much a committee-type government, is that it is going to be in the same position and is going to react in the same way.

I therefore believe that the reasoning which holds that the likelihood of war is going to go up if we deploy missile defenses is wrong. I am among those who argue the other way: We contend that if ABM defenses are deployed, they will at the very least considerably complicate the planning of an attack, and so they must put in a rather substantial additional barrier to the initiation of war.

Let us turn next to the matter of offense-defense arms races. Would the ABM be likely to lead to an unending spiral of defense followed by offense, followed by defense, followed by offense, followed by defense, and so on? I should say the same thing here I said in relation to the argument on the fundamental requirements of deterrence: It ain't necessarily so.

The question is basically one of attitude. If the American body politic defines as a fundamental objective for the Department of Defense that it must have an offensive force capable of killing seventy-four million Russians, without regard to the Soviet capability to kill Americans, and if the Soviets then start building a missile defense that looks as if it would reduce our capability to destroy Russians below that threshold, then, of course, there will be an offensive-force response on our side. The Secretary of Defense would be obliged, in accordance with that dictum, to increase his offensive forces.

Mr. McNamara did precisely that in opposing an incipient Soviet defense by increasing the American offensive forces in response—and indeed, increasing them considerably more than his own estimates of Soviet defensive capabilities required. But it is not, as I said, a fundamental requirement of nature that we must be able to maintain a fixed number of Russians as "hostages." A much more sensible United States posture, it seems to me, in accordance with the dictate of keeping in a good military position vis-à-vis the Soviets, is to deploy ABM defenses here instead. From many points of view, as Dr. Wiesner, I think, perceived, we should have much more interest in deploying defenses than in deploying offensive forces. I think the policy process in the United States will acquire that perspective sooner or later.

I cannot myself discern any fundamental necessity for the United States to respond to Soviet defense build-up with increased offensive-force increments on our side. So far as one can see, Soviet attitudes are themselves already favorable to a defensive posture. While in recent years they have been substantially and sharply increasing their offensive forces, it is still probable that they have more of a doctrinal emphasis on defense as a way of military life than has obtained in the United States in quite a few years. Given that fact, if the United States' attitude went in the direction that I have suggested, and as many other analysts of these matters would suggest, we should find ourselves more or less lined up with the Soviets as to our fundamental missile strategy. We might both come to place primary emphasis on defense, and in that context we might find it very easy to agree to an effective ceiling on offensive forces that would head off the kind of arms race that rightly concerns most students of these matters.

I do not myself treat lightly the prospect of an offense-defense arms race. But I think there is a better way of dealing with it than by abstaining from defense systems, which, as Premier Kosygin rightly put it, will not kill people. The ABM is not intended to kill anything but lethal offensive missiles. It is intended to preserve human lives.

Insofar as both we and the Russians cultivate that judgment (sometimes described as a naive judgment, but, if you look hard at these matters, not so naive) then we can temper the prospects for an arms race and in the process buy a lot of insurance for both the super-powers.

There is no objective barrier that I can see to either the United States' or the Soviet Union's pursuing *this* kind of policy, with respect to the emphasis to be given on the one hand to defense and on the other hand to offense. We can, if we work at it intelligently, have both sound defenses *and* a world free of the apprehensions and waste of a major arms race.

Leon W. Johnson

"If our scientists can build weapons to penetrate enemy defenses, they can build weapons to stop enemy weapons from penetrating our defenses. Too much is at stake to do less."

My response to the question posed in the title of this discussion is a blunt: ABM, yes. That short answer, I think, is best understood in the light of a series of prior questions:

How do you want to live?

Does living under a balance of terror excite and please you?

Are you willing to accept, for all time, a national strategy that means living in fear of the Soviets, not just for today and tomorrow but for the rest of your natural life?

Do you want actions of our government colored primarily by Soviet actions rather than actions based upon a reasoned analysis of what is in the best interests of our country and the best interests of our trusting allies?

Do you want small and insignificant nations seizing our ships upon the high seas?

If you can answer "yes" to those questions, then you must

have reveled in the tense situation and fear of impending doom brought about by the Cuban missile crisis, as we have now seen it described by the late Senator Robert Kennedy.

You must have been excited by the seizure of the Pueblo and waited impatiently for the next act of the drama.

I am not critical of our reactions to these crises; these were trials we had to endure. These were phases in our development, the results of the invention and deployment of new weapons. And it was these new weapons that brought about the balance of terror, resulting in the strategy of "assured destruction," the *only* possible strategy for the present and the immediate future.

My plea is that we do not accept, as a permanent thing, a distorted version of this strategy that will lead to more and bolder confrontations, directly or by proxy, with the Soviets as they match or exceed our nuclear offensive capability. Such a strategy could lead to the subjugation or destruction of our nation if the Soviets should develop an effective strategic defensive force while, at the same time, we were led to believe that a nuclear balance still existed.

The strategy of assured destruction, or deterrence through a balance of terror, means that we must have the capability to destroy the Soviet Union as a viable nation even after suffering a surprise first strike. This is a radically new military concept. Only since the early 1950's have we believed that we must maintain a force-in-being capable of destroying a potential enemy. Prior to that time the planners held that we needed only sufficient force-in-being to defend the country while greater forces were created in order to carry the war to the enemy.

Under those circumstances we never insisted that our forces had to be sufficient to devastate an entire country. The ultimate objective was only to muster sufficient strength to defeat the enemy's forces and destroy his war-making potential. The war would end when the enemy sued for peace, surrendered, and accepted defeat. We assumed that victory would come well short of total destruction; and it has been our practice to lend moral and physical assistance to our enemies in rebuilding and resuming their places in the family of nations. We pride our- selves on being builders, not destroyers.

When the most knowledgeable authorities charged with the defense of our country can say that our strategic offensive and defensive forces have the capability to blunt any enemy attack, to keep the damage to our country to an acceptable level, and to permit us to continue as a viable nation, then we can change back from a strategy of assured destruction to the earlier con- cept of measured damage. It would no longer be essential to destroy an enemy as a viable nation. It would be necessary to inflict only sufficient damage to insure his recognition that the employment of armed force against us was not rewarding and that there are other and better ways to settle international disputes.

Each major weapons change and each spectacular technologi- cal advance leads to changes in the basic strategic principles of war. However, the pendulum swings, although sometimes slowly, and the old laws of force and counterforce, of action and reaction, hold: When the offense outstrips the defense, intensive defensive efforts are applied, and defense is soon back in the picture.

When the nuclear bomb was first exploded, it dwarfed man's concepts and momentarily made him believe that the ultimate weapon had arrived. Then the bomb was placed upon the end of a guided ballistic missile. And another "ultimate" weapon came into view. However, there was soon talk of effective defenses against the simple missile. Decoys and penetration aids were introduced on the offensive side to restore the ICBM to supremacy. But defensive missiles also were making advances; indeed, the knowledge gained in making improvements in the offense has been applied to improving the defense, and vice versa. Thus the never-ending contest has continued even as the contending forces departed the earth and left the atmosphere behind.

The assured-destruction strategy has worked as well as it has because we have had the preponderance of strategic offensive force. However, significant changes have been made in the balance. Within the last three years the Soviets have greatly increased their offensive missile force. And we know that there has been a sharp change in Soviet policy, or at least in our interpretation of that policy. In the spring of 1965 the Secretary of Defense stated that the Soviet leaders "have decided that they have lost the quantitative race, and they are not seeking to engage us in that contest." At that time the Soviets had fewer than 340 intercontinental ballistic missiles, or at least we gave them credit for about that number.

The extent of the change that has taken place is shown by an article appearing in the Washington *Post* last month, wherein Secretary of Defense Clark Clifford used figures showing the United States with 1,054 ICBM's, and the Soviets with 900 ICBM's.

A check of the reports released over the past two years shows that a new ICBM has been added to the Soviet inventory approximately every second day. Any knowledgeable person examining these figures must recognize that the balance of terror is still in full operational effect.

While the figures quoted refer to Soviet strategic offensive weapons, we have the testimony of former Secretary of Defense McNamara early in 1968, which cited the installation of a Soviet ABM system around Moscow and warned that we must "plan our forces on the assumption that they will have deployed some sort of an ABM system around their major cities by the early 1970's."

That the Soviets have a different outlook on ABM's than our own authorities have had is indicated by Mr. Kosygin's statements in London in February 1967. The Washington *Post* reported: "Kosygin distinguished between defensive and offensive weapons and said the latter were less likely to increase international tensions. He admitted that the ABM system was more expensive but said cost could not be a criterion for this decision."

Should the Soviets deploy an ABM system around Moscow and their major cities in the early 1970's, such a condition could be exceedingly destabilizing. Certainly we would not test those defenses. Should the Soviets believe, even mistakenly, that their defenses could blunt an attack of ours, it would be almost as bad for us as if it were true. Should they believe they could blunt an attack with acceptable losses, and so announce to the world, the world would be prone to believe them. It could be expected that many U.S. citizens would also believe them, and the uproar could be much worse than the cry of "missile gap" we experienced in 1960. If we had in the meantime lost the six years of lead time necessary to build and install a defensive system of our own, there would be no way to redress the balance. We would be subject to that Soviet nuclear blackmail we have avoided for the past twenty years.

Now, let us assume that we will continue to operate under an assured-destruction strategy, the offensive concept we are operating under at the present. The principal arguments for the assured-destruction strategy are:

1. It should deter a nuclear attack upon the United States as long as the Soviets believe they will be destroyed by retaliation to such an attack, or until they are convinced the United States is about to launch an attack upon them.
2. It should permit the United States to pursue its foreign policy up to the point of direct confrontation with the Soviets.
3. It should reduce the reasons for an arms race and help to hold within bounds the cost of strategic forces if both sides are convinced that assured destruction can always be maintained.

The arguments against the assured-destruction strategy are:

1. It is not a war-waging strategy and provides no war-termination capability. Should deterrence fail and general nuclear war develop, it can be expected to result in the destruction of the United States as a viable nation.
2. It makes it essential that the United States consider Soviet vital interests most carefully and avoid transgressing them,

recognizing all the while that it is impossible to know exactly what the Soviets consider those interests to be.

3. As the United States strategic offensive forces have little coercive value and little other value except for the deterrence of general nuclear war, other major forces must be provided, or else lack of such forces must be accepted as an important limitation on national policy.

4. It is not a strategy that encourages other nations to ally themselves with the United States, because they could not believe that the United States would support, defend, and save them, regardless of what commitments had been made, if it meant the assured destruction of the United States.

I repeat, the strategy of assured destruction could fail if the Soviets ever believe they have sufficient defensive capability to blunt or make acceptable the damage that a U.S. attack could inflict upon them. A major damage-limiting capability, then, could result in an unbalanced Soviet view of relative deterrence. This could lead to more aggressive Soviet actions and a reduced Soviet willingness to negotiate over misunderstandings. The United States, possessing no important damage-limiting capability for itself, would be under great restraint in all its actions and subject to nuclear blackmail. Assured destruction is a reactive, not a forcing, strategy; the security of the United States and the future of our people and society would be almost completely dependent upon the Soviet Union and to a lesser extent upon Communist China.

Now let us see what the results of adding an effective ballistic-missile defense to our offensive strategic forces could be. The arguments for such a strategy are:

1. It would deter Soviet nuclear attack upon the United States unless the Soviets were convinced that the United States was about to launch an all-out attack upon them.

2. It should produce a war-waging posture that should permit war termination under conditions favorable to the United States.

3. It would permit the United States to pursue its foreign

policy with forthrightness and with consideration, but not compelling fear, of the Soviets.

4. It should permit the United States to use general-purpose forces in limited situations with more freedom of action than does the present policy. The Soviets would have to act with more care in supporting wars of national liberation and in pushing world revolution, or in employing direct conventional military pressures.

5. Should over-all deterrence fail, it would give the President the option of a flexible response rather than a spasm response, as the nation would not lie naked to the Soviet attack. Our weapons and our control systems would have more chance of survival for use as needed.

6. It might lead the Soviets to a more reasonable attitude toward meaningful arms-control measures because the great relative wealth and economic capability of the United States, when applied to the task of developing a greater security position, might convince the Soviet leaders of the folly of challenging us further in the arms race and make them turn their attention to less threatening forms of competition.

The arguments against this strategy are:

1. It may be that it is not technologically attainable at the moment. However, it is certain that the present ABM potential could reduce the damage that the United States might suffer. It should be able to provide national entity survival and let us survive as a nation for a period before it attains the capability of reducing casualties to a large extent here.

2. It might engage the United States in an all-out arms race with the Soviets, which could be expensive both in dollars and in talent. However, it is a race that we should be able to win, and the race may in fact be in progress at the moment.

We can only consider those strategic arguments in the light of contemporary political reality. The world situation has not stood still. The Soviets, through increased activities in the Middle East and in the Mediterranean and by their repressive actions in Czechoslovakia, appear to be serving notice upon us that they consider a new day to have dawned. It appears that they are less concerned with Western reactions. They move when they believe it to be to their advantage.

The New York Times of October 29, 1968, reported that General Lemnitzer, the Supreme Allied Commander in Europe, has said that the Soviet-led invasion of Czechoslovakia was a "complete tactical surprise" and tipped the European power balance in favor of the communist countries.

Admiral McCain, the recent American Naval Commander in Europe, has warned that the Soviet Navy is building up a strong capability in the Mediterranean. The Los Angeles *Times,* on November 12, 1968, quoted from the official Soviet government newspaper *Izvestia:*

"The Mediterranean should be turned into a sea of peace. This can be achieved only by active struggle against American imperialism whose political and military system in the Mediterranean Sea should be liquidated."

Izvestia criticized plans for the creation of a North Atlantic Treaty Organization naval force with headquarters in Naples.

These seem to be examples of Soviet restlessness and eagerness to let the world know that they have interests in all the world's areas.

Our capability for assured destruction seems to have little dissuasive value when such Soviet moves are contemplated, even when we warn that results could have a decided disadvantage in terms of our national interests.

The world's technical and scientific capability has not reached a plateau. If our scientists can build weapons to penetrate enemy defenses, they can build weapons to stop enemy weapons from penetrating our defenses.

Too much is at stake to do less.

When the official military publication of the Soviet Union, edited by Marshal V. D. Sokolovsky, contains such a preposterous statement as, "Imperialist countries openly proclaim their mad plans to liquidate the Soviet Union and other Socialist countries through a new world war," and when it adds such statements as, "Taking this into account . . . the party is taking all steps to strengthen the defensive powers of our motherland and to increase the combat readiness of the Soviet armed forces," it must be apparent how little we understand each other.

Until there is a better understanding and a meeting of the minds, our military posture must be one of strength across the board. Our military posture cannot be complete without a defense against Soviet missiles.

It is time to recall that a strategy based on self-interest includes, *ipso facto*, the defense of population regardless of the other side's statements, intentions, or reactions. Failure to realize this will in the long run be tremendously constraining, destabilizing, and costly to our foreign policy and could cause the death of our great country.

Finally, we all would join in the hope that both the Soviets and ourselves will continue to operate under a policy of deterrence long after our weapons of offense and defense have been retired for old age. However, this deterrence does not mean a United States helpless in the face of Soviet nuclear blackmail, but, as Richard Foster of Stanford Research Institute says, "a deterrence which permits the continuance of unhindered access to other free countries, a deterrence which permits the fundamental rights of freedom of the seas, international air ways, and inner as well as outer space."

The Colloquy

After making the foregoing statements, Messrs. Wiesner, Mc-Govern, Brennan, and Johnson were joined in a discussion by Adolf A. Berle, Freeman Dyson, Charles M. Herzfeld, I. I. Rabi, H. Franz Schurmann and Center Fellows Harry S. Ashmore, W. H. Ferry, Neil H. Jacoby, and Harvey Wheeler.

Disagreement by the Numbers

BRENNAN: I think I can demonstrate that Senator McGovern has not done all his homework. It is not cheap to nullify a good defense. As far as we can see, the reverse of that case has been a technical prospect for four or five years. I do not know of a serious study, classified or unclassified, anywhere, that suggests that it is presently cheaper to nullify a good defense than it is to build one. Senator McGovern repeated the standard shibboleth when he said that the Soviets could nullify a defense of ours for a smaller outlay than was required to install it. He says we did this when we extended our offensive force in responding to the new Soviet defense system. I would guess that the United States has committed about five times the cost of the Soviet defense in order to neutralize it.

The Senator uses the figure of $3.2 billion for the Poseidon program. And the Minuteman III program costs about $2 billion, depending on how many missiles are deployed. So it's about a $5-billion program that Secretary McNamara laid down in offensive-force response to about a $1-billion Soviet missile defense. Nobody knows for sure, of course, whether the Soviet defense system cost $1 billion, or $800 million, or $2 billion; but it is a small and modest system, and the offset, the neutralization of it that was programmed by Mr. McNamara, was several times as costly as that defense. Now, of course, what has been programmed in Poseidon and Minuteman III will, in fact, offset a much more substantial defense if the Soviets put one in.

Senator McGovern also said that the heavy ABM system is no match for Poseidon. That is not a point the Defense Department would agree with. It is certain, of course, that if the Soviets put in something like the Poseidon program, and if we put in what Dr. Wiesner earlier alluded to as the Posture B system, some of those Poseidon-type warheads could get through; but an awful lot of them could not. We are talking here in statistics, but these statistics may well be important for the survival of something we think of as the United States. In the survival sense, the heavy ABM system may very well be a match for Poseidon. And if the Soviets put in a like defense, then it's not at all obvious that the five billion dollars or so we have already committed to offensive forces would indeed neutralize that larger program.

The final point I want to make is that it is not obvious that we should want to increase our offensive forces this way. I would argue that the $5 billion that has already been committed to an offensive-force response to the Soviet defense would have been much better spent on a U.S. defense that would not raise the level of Soviet hostages. Spending for defense might degrade our deterrence somewhat, but it would certainly reduce very much the number of American hostages to Soviet offensive forces. And we would not have enhanced the possibility of beginning an offense-defense arms race if we had chosen that other direction, the direction of defense.

WIESNER: I would like to clarify what I think Senator McGovern said. He was comparing the Sentinel, that Edsel of ABM's, with the Poseidon. But of course he could have said that we did not have to buy the Poseidon to offset a Sentinel-type ABM defense. The original Polaris missile was more than a match for such a defense. The Polaris missile, with two thirds of the fleet at home, would still have been a match for the Sentinel. I think all the offensive missiles on the test range are probably a match for the Sentinel. I think the Sentinel is totally useless. I think most of the experts generally admit that now. So if the Sentinel, which also costs $5 billion, is not a match for our existing offensive systems, we did not have to spend a nickel to improve them.

But Senator McGovern's basic point is certainly true. The Poseidon deployment would undoubtedly overwhelm the Sentinel system. Would half the Poseidon overwhelm the Sentinel, Mr. Brennan?

BRENNAN: I would hate to quote some of the estimates I have heard of what would be required to overwhelm the Sentinel.

WIESNER: All right. So you can give any ratio you want here, 50-to-1 or 10-to-1; the ratio doesn't have to be that extreme. But I think the Sentinel will always end up on the losing end.

Dr. Brennan said one thing, which he seemed to suggest we were in agreement on, which I thought was just the opposite of what I was trying to say. He interpreted me to be suggesting that there are many ways to make a good anti-missile defense. I was not saying that at all. I said that it is conceivable that some genius might invent a totally different kind of defensive system, one not dependent on shooting things up in the air and setting off nuclear weapons, and therefore one that will be more effective than the kind we are now making. The key point here is that so long as we are dependent on the present mode, I do not think we will ever make a defensive system that can win out against the offense. To depart from this mode, as an example, maybe somebody could make a strong enough laser beam or a strong enough nuclear power beam of some kind. But I was not suggesting these are possible. They are very unlikely. And that is a significant measure of how tough this problem is, rather than how easy I think it is.

Just to add to the list of offensive possibilities—I did mention multiple warheads and decoys—both the United States and the Soviet Union have developed very large nuclear explosions. I think both by now have rockets that can carry this increased capacity. I think our C-5 rocket could probably carry a fifty-thousand- or a hundred-thousand-pound payload to the Soviet Union. I suspect their rockets could bring something like that here. So both sides have the possibility, if either wanted to do it, of setting off enormous bombs at very high altitudes and generating all kinds of interesting effects.

One of the things that became clear in all the calculation made on the Nike-Zeus—and I suspect its's also true of the very interesting calculations Mr. McNamara cites in his 1967 Defense Posture statement—is that nobody paid adequate attention to the heat effects; low-altitude explosions set off thermofluxes that could ignite much of the ignitable structures below. It is probably true that the bombs in the new system are smaller and may not give this effect, but I suspect there is more there than has been taken into account.

And we forget, if General Johnson has not forgotten, the airplane. The United States still has six hundred bombers. It is estimated that about half of those would get through to their targets. That sounds like a fairly effective deterrent. But we always leave this prime factor out of the calculations. Whenever I mention this around the Pentagon, I get the dirty look usually reserved for people who drag a dead horse into the living room. The fact is that the Soviets, for a whole series of reasons—industrial, technical, strategic—never built quite the air force we did. But they do have a few hundred long-range bombers—a couple of hundred, anyway. And we never built quite as good an air defense system as they did, partly because it is tougher for us since a lot of our strategic targets are on the coasts. In any event, I do not think anyone would claim that we are totally invulnerable to the old Soviet Air Force, and they certainly aren't to ours.

There are a lot of other unmentioned possibilities that complicate this issue. We could even go back to a big program of modern airplanes for nuclear delivery. The Air Force has been trying to do just that for years. They just haven't been able to design the right airplane, or at least they couldn't convince Mr. McNamara that they had. (He didn't design a very good one, either.) But I suspect that one could do better in that regard with a little encouragement.

Let me turn to just one other point. General Johnson's statement about the problem we have with regard to the Russians does not seem to me to take sufficiently into account the maneuverability we have in controlling the arms race, or even our responsibility for contributing to it. When I was a little boy and first began to play with these toys, working at the M.I.T. radiation laboratory, I believed everything I was told. I spent the 1950's working very hard on air defense, on missiles, on a variety of things, because I was told by my superiors that the Russians were ahead of us, that they were working against the day when they would get enough power to carry out a surprise attack and wipe us out. This, it was said, was their only purpose in life.

Then we graduated from that to the missile gap, which, in fact, I had helped to invent. Then it became clear that many of us had just misinterpreted the signals. Eventually, when we got enough information, we saw two things: First, the Russians had opted out of the bomber race quite early in the game—they never built a bomber force capable of wiping out our force or doing the other things we said they wanted to do and could do; and second, for a long time they were prepared to settle for a missile force considerably smaller than ours.

Then, at some point a few years ago, the Russians decided to build more missiles, and they are now drawing equal. I hope they are only drawing equal. I hope they don't intend to double what we have, because if they do, we obviously will respond. I don't know why the Russians began to build more missiles.

Maybe it stems from their embarrassment over the Cuban missile crisis. Maybe it stems from their embarrassment at having Mr. McNamara stand up in the Congress every time he had to explain why he was not buying more missiles—that the United States already has four times as many as the Russians. Whatever their motivations, the Russians began adding to their missiles.

This is a point that I think is very important, and one that General Johnson seemed not to appreciate adequately when he said we might wake up one day and discover that the Soviets had made a defensive system that rendered our offensive system inoperative. I have been trying to say that nothing like this is in the cards with these massive, expensive, hard-to-build, hard-to-deploy, hard-to-train-people-to-operate systems. This is real protection. Our information is good enough, and the time lags are such that long before a ballistic-missile defense system could be deployed to protect enough of the Soviet Union to make any difference, we could sail past them, just as we did in the case of offensive missiles.

In any event, now that we have led the Soviet Union in this new weaponry for years, I think it might be an interesting experiment to see whether we couldn't cool this whole business off by slowly cutting down on the numbers we all live by.

Dr. Brennan pointed out correctly that if we build a defensive system that cut in half the number of missiles that fell on our country, it would certainly cut down the damage to our country. I don't know how many Soviet missiles are targeted on New York City at this moment. I'd be very surprised if it is fewer than ten; maybe it is more. And it only takes one to do a pretty good job on a city, even one this size.

But instead of building these defensive systems and proving that I am right and Dr. Brennan is wrong about the way the response will come, why not get the same effect by cutting down on the number of offensive missiles? That is the other way to do this. I think it would work. You wouldn't have to cut them in half right away, although I don't think that would matter; I don't think you would be able to tell the difference. But you could cut down a little bit. And we could say to the Soviets: "We will cut down a little more if you will cut down a little more." Let's see whether we both, the United States and the U.S.S.R., can race in the other direction, and see who can count the most empty holes on the launching sites ten years from now.

Is Airtight Defense Possible?

JOHNSON: I would like to ask Senator McGovern this: If we could build for a reasonable figure a ballistic-missile defense that he felt would insure the survival of the country, would he vote to build that ballistic-missile defensive system?

McGOVERN: Yes, if there were a way to build an airtight system that would put a country in a genuinely secure position, I think both the Soviets and the United States ought to build it, and any other nation who can afford it. But that is not possible. The thrust of my argument, and I think this has been the thrust of Secretary McNamara's argument from the very beginning, is that this is not what happens when you build a defensive system. The other side promptly counters it by increasing its capacity to penetrate the new defenses. So we're postulating something that is just not in the cards.

I have suggested that we keep alive the research programs looking for the kind of a breakthrough General Johnson predicates in his question. If the day ever comes when it looks as if we've found a foolproof defense, why it might be wise to go ahead and deploy it. But I see nothing in present proposals to indicate that likelihood.

In regard to Dr. Brennan's statement, the point I was trying to make about the conversion of the Polaris to the Poseidon missile system is that for a little over $3 billion we were able to convert 600 warheads to 4,000. Presumably it will now take 4,000 defensive warheads to knock them all down. Now, that's about the capacity we will get for the $20 billion Secretary McNamara estimated for the so-called Posture B defense, which is the heavy ABM defense system.

The offensive system we got when we stepped up Polaris to Poseidon for $3 billion has developed enough firepower to obliterate the entire Soviet Union and the rest of the world several times over. We built all this on the theory that the Soviets might be putting in a heavy ABM system. It turns out instead that they were installing a kind of half-baked system around Moscow alone. And that's all, that one system, plus a dubious bomber-defense system around Leningrad. That's the extent of the ABM system against which we have arrayed all this additional striking power.

On the basis of that one little scare about what they were doing with their defenses around Moscow, we have already overbuilt on the offensive side to provide a capacity that could pulverize the entire country many times over. No one can deny that they can do the same thing to us if they are moved to. So I must reject the argument that we are buying additional security when we go down this so-called defensive route of deploying what very well may prove to be an ABM sieve through which offensive missiles can still pour in devastating volume.

How Many Fatalities Would Be Fatal?

BERLE: I do not think the anti-ballistic-missile system should be deployed. I think the research on it should be done and the information acquired but that we should stop there. I can find no technician who is prepared to say that an anti-ballistic-missile defense could be airtight. One argument for deploying an ABM system is that it could reduce the number of our fatalities to ten or fifteen million. But we have no way of determining whether we could sustain ten or fifteen million deaths without having our whole social, governmental, and political system smashed and our country so disorganized that it would be brought to the point of defeat. So until someone is prepared to tell us that an anti-ballistic-missile system can prevent even that "slight" penetration by an enemy, I do not think we can assume the ABM would be effective.

BRENNAN: There is general agreement among technically informed people that if we spent from ten to twenty billions for the ABM, it would reduce fatality levels from perhaps fifty per cent of the population to ten or fifteen per cent, and it probably would save an even greater percentage of our industrial resources. This would be true in the kind of war that could happen in the middle or late 1970's, pitting the ABM against advanced technology skillfully employed in more or less optimum ways against the United States. It is a combination of these two reductions that, in the judgment of many people who have studied recovery problems, would indeed make the difference between having a country that could reconstitute itself within some relatively modest number of years (say, five or ten) after the war, and having a country whose recovery in any time period would be highly problematical.

FERRY: In these calculations, should one add a factor for survivors who are burned, wounded, made ill?

BRENNAN: The figures from former Defense Secretary McNamara's 1967 Defense Posture statement are for fatalities only; that is, deaths from prompt blast and fallout activity. I should add that many people believe that when you have substantial defenses operating, there is a much better chance of dealing with the survivors. If you lose, say, half the people and three fourths or seven eighths of a country's resources, it is much harder to take care of survivors.

McGOVERN: Do you feel that Secretary McNamara is the most reliable source of information about the reduction in fatalities if we were to deploy an ABM?

BRENNAN: Mr. McNamara is known to have been one of the most intense critics of anti-ballistic-missile defenses for the last several years. It is not to be expected that his estimates on fatalities would be biased in favor of the defensive system.

HERZFELD: I've looked at a large fraction of the numbers of this sort and at the examples given in Mr. McNamara's testimony and by other people. While there are wide ranges, of course, depending upon the assumptions one uses, these numbers are typical and fairly represent the best state of our understanding.

WIESNER: Would it be fair to take these numbers and characterize them this way? That if we build a $20-billion ABM system and if it functions just as the designers predict it will—namely, if everything is going to work, the thousands of GI's who man the launching sites are going to be ready, the computer programming is going to be right, there are no surprises in the incoming missiles, and the tremendous battle that takes place in the skies does not produce such chaos and blackout that everything quits working (all reasons why I think it will not work)—then the casualties would be reduced to fifteen per cent of our population, or 30 million people? So that the truth of these numbers and estimates lies somewhere between what I think is a very optimistic 30 million deaths and, at the upper end, 120 million deaths based on what we project the Russians could do against no defenses? It comes down, then, to a matter of somebody's judgment, because there is no way of knowing what the Soviets are going to do, and there is no way of knowing how the ABM system is going to function. We would be absolute fools if we predicated our behavior on an assumption of ideal performance of everything that goes into the design of an ABM system.

BERLE: The debate on numbers is immaterial. The question is whether even the most optimistic estimate of fatalities means the smashing of the central nervous system of our whole society.

WIESNER: I think you are absolutely right. A sudden death of 30 million people, or even 10 million, would so disrupt this country that it would panic.

BERLE: So, even accepting the low estimates of fatalities by defense protagonists, unless that defense were so airtight that one could be sure the country was essentially protected, that defense would not be adequate.

BRENNAN: The optimistic estimates of the results of an

ABM defense are based on the assumption that the Soviet offensive force also performs exactly as expected.

WIESNER: If you have a ten per cent failure in a defensive system in a thermonuclear war, you have a catastrophe. A ten per cent failure in the offensive system is not nearly so serious. So, if you want to talk about symmetry in the reliability figures for both offensive and defensive performance, the symmetry is not absolute; it is relative and must be adjusted to fit this reality.

The Argument for Thin Defense

HERZFELD: I'm in favor of a thin anti-ballistic-missile defense, the original Sentinel with some important but relatively cheap improvements. I am against the thick defense mainly because I think it buys too little for the dollars. The thin defense does some important things for one in the prewar stage, whereas no defense that I can think of would do very much for one in an all-out war with the Soviet Union.

A thin defense does rather well against unsophisticated attacks. (In spite of what is said and printed, it is not easy, cheap, or quick for an unsophisticated technology to produce a sophisticated offense.) The thin defense is extremely helpful in all third-country problems, and as time goes on there are going to be third countries with nuclear capacity other than the Chinese People's Republic. In addition, a thin defense system buys very good insurance against accidental attacks.

A thin defense also can provide a firebreak at a very high level of tension, a level even more intense than that of the Cuban missile crisis. At such a level, if an antagonist who's really not very serious about war wants to blackmail you by firing one, two, or five demonstration shots, a thin defense robs his threat of reality. A thin defense is like having a very high ante for a poker game; it keeps out the people who are not serious.

The notion of a thin defense did not suddenly come up in 1967. The matter has been studied since 1962. Sentinel is not a highly speculative system. It is based on much more than "studies," though many studies went into Nike and Sentinel. But there are lots of measurements in the field—thorough, complete measurements that are used to synthesize estimates of what would happen.

WIESNER: I think it is a general technical consensus that Sentinel is not going to buy us any protection against a Soviet missile attack. I don't believe there is anybody here who would argue that it is. So the question of what the Sentinel does as far as a U.S.–U.S.S.R. nuclear confrontation is concerned is irrelevant. One might then ask, "Well, why do you care whether or not Sentinel is built?" I care because I think it is regarded by most advocates of anti-ballistic-missile systems as the down payment on a much more substantial system. I have heard high-ranking officers say that if they thought the Sentinel system was all that the United States ever intended to buy, they would be against it. But they believe that it will lead naturally to the large-scale system. It is then appropriate to ask whether deployment of a large-scale anti-ballistic-missile system would, in fact, add to or detract from national security. My judgment is that in the end we would, at best, be in very little different posture than we are now but with a military system a great deal bigger; and that, at worst, we would be in a situation in which the actual damage could be somewhat greater.

Balance of Terror?

JOHNSON: I am not sure we are facing up to the question. I think the question is: Are we satisfied with the strategy of deterrence, of assured destruction, both now and for the future? I am convinced that this strategy does not meet our requirements. A capability for mutual destruction of the United States and the U.S.S.R.—a destruction I hope will never take place—is one that leaves us at a distinct disadvantage for our day-to-day operations because of the accident of geography and the fact that we have commitments and alliances around the world.

Operating within the framework of the present deterrence or assured-mutual-destruction strategy, the United States can be inhibited from taking the actions and using the weapons that might be most effective. This is because the United States does not want to risk escalation to a level that might get out of control.

In the Cuban missile crisis we were fearful of the holocaust although really the Soviets at that time had little capability against us. They could not have killed us; they could have damaged us seriously at that time, but we could have overwhelmingly killed them.

The Secretary of Defense in 1965, with the best intelligence available to him, was misled about the Russians' challenge to us in the intercontinental-ballistic-missile race. A year later, the Soviets had started building their ICBM forces. What I fear now is that we will be misled about the extent and capacity of Soviet defenses. I am not a scientist, so I can neither agree nor disagree with Dr. Wiesner when he assures us that long before the Russians could deploy an ABM system, we would be able to take adequate countermeasures. There is a possibility he may be wrong. The Department of Defense was wrong once before. If we wait for Russia to start an ABM system, we may not have time to catch up, and then we will be subject to nuclear blackmail.

The Soviets do not need a completely effective ABM system for the improvement of their defenses to have a disastrous effect on us. If the Soviets *believe* they have an adequate system, even though it is quite inadequate, that may be sufficient to launch them on new adventures. I believe we should make a policy of our own, not accept this standoff which means living under a balance of terror. We should get on with building our defenses up to a point where we know we can continue the type of life we want for this country.

DYSON: I would like to ask why the objections that have been raised against the Sentinel system were not raised against our MIRV (multiple independently targetable re-entry vehicles), against our Poseidon system, and against our Minuteman

III when the decision was made to deploy those offensive systems. Poseidon and Minuteman III have properties that make them very much more dangerous and very much more escalatory than the Sentinel system. First, these new offensive systems vastly increase the number of warheads targeted on our opponents, who perceive them as being directly threatening; so that, politically speaking, such offensive systems are much more likely to lead to an intensified arms race.

Second, these new offensive systems lead to a situation where both sides have, or might be feared to have, first-strike capability, but where one now has a sufficient number of warheads to attack all the opponent's launchers with some prospect of putting them out of action. In such a situation both sides would feel very much more strongly threatened than otherwise.

Finally, we should not underestimate the danger that the Polaris system as a whole may turn out to be vulnerable if, say, the Soviet Union feels itself to be critically threatened by these four thousand Poseidon warheads on the submarines. The Soviet Union may feel itself driven to take direct action against the Polaris system in peacetime. This is a danger that I think we should all wish to avoid like the plague.

WIESNER: I raised my voice and fought very hard against MIRV. I tried during last spring to get the Senate to recognize what was involved in both the MIRV's and Minuteman III. I think these, too, are foolish investments. I think that doing the research and development and having the capability to use such weapons *if* they appeared to be necessary in the event of an effective Soviet deployment of ABM's would have made a certain amount of sense. But in my opinion both MIRV and Minuteman III were provocative and unnecessary at this stage.

JACOBY: Will the ABM escalate the arms race? Will it impede progress toward disarmament? My conclusion is that the ABM is as likely to help as it is to hurt. But I don't think the evidence is unambiguous on either side.

WIESNER: General Johnson and Dr. Jacoby have raised, in different ways, a central question. I think all of us would agree with General Johnson that we do not like to live under a mutual annihilation threat, the balance of terror, as he terms it. The question is: How do we get out from under? General Johnson assumes that if we work hard enough at defense, we can build some kind of electronic barrier, what I have called an electronic Maginot Line. I am convinced that the offense can stay ahead of the defense on either or both sides if the governments elect to do so. Involved here, then, is one's judgment about what nations will choose to do.

My own experience with decision-making in these matters—decision-making, for example, in the Department of Defense, which is always under very real pressures from the Congress—is that the political process will always force the decision-making in the direction of sufficient offense to insure the effectiveness of our own terror. So I do not accept the proposition that escalation of defenses might stabilize the situation. If I thought it would, I would buy it.

I come back, then, to Dr. Jacoby's concern about de-escalation. I believe very strongly that we must try to de-escalate the arms race, that we must try first to freeze and then to eliminate, to the extent that we can, offensive nuclear forces. When we had relatively small nuclear forces with the capability of killing "only" twenty million people on each side, we were probably no worse off than we are today. Perhaps we can work our way back down to that level of destructive capacity.

The real question is whether the deployment of some kind of anti-ballistic-missile system will enhance or detract from our ability to achieve a strategic offensive-weapons limitation and possible reduction. One can argue on both sides of this, as we have been doing. If there were some kind of thin defense system in existence, and if it were frozen and there was no prospect that it would be built up into a thick system, it might provide a nice umbrella at some stage in international relations. Once you got rid of most of the offensive missiles, then this thin defense system would be a comfortable thing to have; it would eliminate the threat to your security from clandestine weapons. But I do not believe that in the present context one can start out to build an ABM system and at the same time press ahead to freeze and reduce offensive strategic forces. On the other hand, I think one can undertake a considerable reduction of offensive power of the kind Dr. Jacoby is talking about without any anti-ballistic-missile system at all.

As a strong advocate of mutual arms limitation and disarmament I have asked myself over and over again whether there are circumstances under which deployment of an ABM system would help us reach those objectives. I always end up concluding that they do not, and cannot, exist.

BRENNAN: Dr. Wiesner and I have a fundamental disagreement on what these pressures are that he says are pushing up offensive forces. There are indeed upward pressures on the offensive side, pressures on behalf of various perceptions of what is required for national security. It is my belief that these pressures could be at least as well, and probably better, satisfied by pushing up the level of defense—letting the defense capacity go up on both sides, thereby reducing the scale of the disaster nuclear war would bring to both parties. I believe these pressures can be turned into a force on behalf of active defense instead of a force working to increase offensive capacity on both sides, carrying with it the literal threat of world-wide destruction. This is the point where we do have a fundamental disagreement.

WHEELER: That is why the argument, then, comes down basically to a nontechnical, experimental, and psychological question: What is A likely to do if B does such-and-so?

ASHMORE: In this connection, I am reminded of a conversation with Secretary McNamara early in 1967—some months before he yielded in his opposition to the ABM. I had just returned from Hanoi, and the purpose of the meeting was to report to the Secretary on the prospects for a negotiated settlement in Vietnam. But it was clear that our difficulties in Southeast Asia, even though they would soon bring down the Administration he served, had second priority among his concerns.

The world would survive the worst that could happen in Vietnam, he said, but it might not survive the shifting views among the military leaders—on our side and on that of the

Soviets. Important people in high places, Mr. McNamara said, are arguing that they can find technical means of using thermonuclear missiles and still survive—and thereby win. He felt that this is the most disastrous concept that could possibly gain currency in the contemporary situation.

This seems to me to be a central point in this whole debate. If there are some among us, and some on the other side, who believe that a system can be set up that will make it possible to use thermonuclear missiles and still win a military victory, then I presume with Secretary McNamara that the danger point is in fact here.

Escalation—Who Is to Blame?

JACOBY: I think we should recognize that the United States is responding to the communist countries, not the reverse. The two initiatives that have disturbed the nuclear balance were taken by the Communists: the deployment by the Soviets of a light defense system around Moscow and perhaps around other centers; and the testing by Communist China of a ballistic missile with intercontinental potentialities.

WIESNER: One has to look at what the Soviets deployed, though. We must try to understand it in context. And we must look even farther back in matters of this kind. It is true that we are responding to the Chinese development of a nuclear bomb. But it is also true that their development of a nuclear bomb was a response to our development of a nuclear bomb and to our use of it. It was the United States that initiated the development of anti-ballistic-missile systems; we began the first research and development, and we began to talk publicly about what we were doing. I have some reason to believe that our early publications guided the Russians in their initial ABM research and development. What they actually deployed around Moscow, as far as we can tell, is still part of a research and development program rather than a massive ABM system of the kind we are talking about on our side.

McGOVERN: What is the evidence that the Soviets are going

beyond this very limited defensive system deployed around Moscow and their apparent aircraft defenses around Leningrad? Do we have credible evidence that they are moving ahead on a nationwide defensive missile system?

BRENNAN: I think the evidence is both ambiguous and undiscussable.

WIESNER: But mostly negative.

HERZFELD: Their system around Moscow is comparable to a thin defense.

WIESNER: No, it is only a small piece of a thin system.

HERZFELD: It's not all that small.

WIESNER: It is.

What Can the Country Afford?

BRENNAN: You know, in a fundamental sense the notion of ballistic-missile defense is scarcely a radical one. And the cost of an ABM system is not out of line when one considers what this country has spent over the last eighteen years trying to put up some kind of an air defense against Soviet bombers. In terms of 1968 dollars the United States investment for the air defense system alone is probably on the order of fifty billion dollars. That does not count replacement cost for parts of the system. Today we're talking of spending about half that much on the investment cost in missile defense.

It is interesting to compare the expected performance of the two systems in terms of what they would buy in the way of insurance. The Soviet bomber threat against which our air defense was deployed probably could never have inflicted more than a few tens of millions of fatalities if we had had no air defense at all. (I hate to use phrases like "only a few tens of millions of fatalities," but they are relevant.) Today the fatality level from a Soviet ballistic-missile attack against an undefended United States would be much, much higher.

The effectiveness of our air defense system during most of these past eighteen years is believed to have been substantially less than the projected effectiveness of the proposed missile defense system. In part this difference derives from the fact that we did not have a comparable research and development program for our air defenses—did not spend some hundreds of millions of dollars over several years trying to find out in advance the holes in our air defense system before it was deployed. If we had done this in the intensive fashion we have looked for flaws in a missile defense system, the ratio might have been different. But as it is, I would say that the fifty billion dollars spent on air defense purchased an awful lot less insurance for our country than it is likely to obtain in the near future with a missile defense system.

BERLE: While, as I have said, I am against ABM deployment because I do not think it will be effective, I do not agree with some critics of the ABM who say that economically the country cannot afford it. That is nonsense. The maximum estimate is that an ABM system would cost $50 billion. The United States can afford that and more. This year the Gross National Product will be about $860 billion. The best estimate for the 1969 G.N.P. is $910 billion. And we can assume that before the ABM would be fully deployed three or four years from now, the G.N.P. would be about a trillion dollars. To detach $50 billion of that G.N.P. for the ABM could be done. It could be done even while we're spending great amounts of money for the social and economic reconstruction of the country. It is true that this would require a political mood of urgency the country does not now have. But economically the ABM is a manageable proposition.

It does no good to underestimate the economic capacity of the United States, which is far greater than the public realizes. On the economic side, then, there appears to be no good argument against the ABM. The real argument against it is that it appears to be waste, as Nike-Zeus would have been waste in its time.

JACOBY: There is a question here about the transferability of the resources allocated to an ABM program. Could the resources released from the Sentinel system be used to help solve some of our domestic problems—urban blight, transportation, poverty? Another question: If Sentinel should be canceled and later the communist powers do move into a heavy anti-ballistic-missile defense, how seriously would we be handicapped by the time required to remobilize our research, development, and production for an ABM? It seems to me there is a weighty argument in favor of having at all times the resources that can be used quickly to develop a missile defense. I agree with Mr. Berle that the real constraint upon our attack on domestic problems is not lack of economic resources, but lack of knowledge and will.

WIESNER: I agree in principle with Dr. Berle. But as I said before, I was against the R&D appropriations for MIRV and Minuteman III because, among other reasons, I thought they were a foolish investment. The money was being spent for them at a time when the government, in practice, did not seem able to squeeze enough dollars out of the economy for our domestic problems. I thought those military investments were deferrable.

McGOVERN: I couldn't agree with Mr. Berle more. This country can probably afford, in sheer economic terms, an expenditure of the kind needed for the ABM. But the political realities are that if we decide to spend major public funds for arms, something else is going to get cut. That is just a political fact of life. In order to fund the Vietnam War this year we were told we had to put through a ten per cent tax increase and at the same time cut six billion dollars out of very essential domestic programs. This was a process of weakening our country. We have been denying funds for a good many things we ought to be doing in education, in resource development, in eliminating air and water pollution. Neglecting these problems presents enormous dangers to the security and well-being of the United States. The threats we face are not all military—but you know how the priorities fall out.

If one argues that we can afford both arms and domestic programs, it does not follow that we would not be far better off if we could find a way to get along with the Russians so that we would not need to spend ninety billion dollars a year on military outlays. The question then becomes one of whether two great countries like the United States and the Soviet Union can even settle their differences in a rational manner while both are armed to the teeth.

RABI: There is no question that we can afford both guns and butter, no question in terms of cold economic statistics. But I am not so sure that economic statistics are a sufficient measurement of what a country can afford. The example of France should give us pause. A year ago France was riding high. She had gold. NATO was a plaything in her hands. She had possessions. She was a going concern. Then her internal troubles developed last spring. Now France is a shambles.

A country is more than its economic capacity or its material possessions. It has a personal, spiritual, psychological side—it is a culture.

Those of us who are teachers are close to young people. We know the degree to which young people have been alienated by all this expenditure on military things. When they see the government putting out tremendous sums of money for military purposes and then observe the government's reluctance to invest in the solution of domestic human problems, they see a reorientation of our national policy that they believe is turning us into a garrison state. If I have any trust in the American people, I can't believe they will stand for it much longer—especially the young people.

I have to say that I find all these statistical arguments, all this war gaming, sort of obscene. It has nothing to do with the meaning of security on a much more profound level. While we are trying to assure the safety of the country, we may be undermining it.

WIESNER: The question of costs and what a country can afford must also include, I think, the psychoses that may be developed and may profoundly affect the way political leaders can function. In a sense, the management of our country has had to live in a psychotic state for a number of years, and this has determined its ability to attack serious domestic problems. I know from firsthand experience that both President Eisenhower and President Kennedy were never able to devote sufficient attention to domestic issues. They were spending most of their time on external matters while also trying to cope with internal pressures on behalf of various aspects of the arms program.

When I worked in the White House, we felt we were beleaguered on several sides, that we were fighting a three- or four-front war. The Soviet front often seemed the most tractable and least threatening, probably because the Russians were so much farther away than our other antagonists, and because the time scale in dealing with the problems they posed was so much greater. I do not think one can overestimate the very adverse effect an unstable arms-race situation can have on the ability of the leaders of our nation to give proper attention to urgent domestic problems. The dollar cost of the ABM—whether we're talking about twenty billion dollars or forty billion—is trivial compared to these other costs.

The Human Equation

RABI: I want to tell you a story that reveals how I feel about all of this. It involves a great mathematician at the University of Göttingen in Germany, and it goes back to 1917, during World War I. This professor had a call from the rector of the university asking him to appear at his home that evening. He had no hint what it was about. But he thought about it all day and finally came to the conclusion that, since this was a time of great famine in Germany, the rector had probably gone out into the country and somehow or other had got hold of a pig, and they would have a feast that evening. This intuition was reinforced when the professor arrived at the rector's home and found other eminent professors of the university already assembled there. Then, precisely at seven o'clock, the rector came in and said: "Gentlemen, I called you all together because I have the pleasure of announcing to you the beginning of unrestricted submarine warfare." The professor said later, "At that moment,

I felt I was living among madmen and that my only safety lay in imitating them down to the last detail."

I don't go all the way with the professor at Göttingen, but I do feel that his reaction is not entirely inappropriate to the discussion we have been having. This is a discussion that has been going on for the last twenty-three years in exactly the same way: the mathematics of first strike, second strike, force and counterforce, is it twenty billion or forty billion dollars, thirty million or eighty million deaths?

When Mr. Eisenhower was President of Columbia University, he said something that struck me. He had never been interested in defending property or even lives, he said, as much as he had in defending a way of life. When you look at the proposition inherent in a nuclear exchange, you realize that even minimal losses—say, taking out New York, Chicago, and Los Angeles and letting everything else stand—would spell the end of the American dream as we know it. And that must be what this whole exercise is all about.

It seems to me that somehow or other we have missed our priorities in the last twenty-three years. We have been using the cream of the technical brains of the country in this general objective of insuring parity in a nuclear exchange, without making any comparable effort or taking any comparable chances to find an alternative means of dealing with international tensions, problems, and differences.

I submit that in our discussions with the Russians we have never really come to terms with them. At the time when the Baruch Plan was put forward after World War II, I think our nation instinctively understood the nature of the problem and recognized the need to rely on something other than a nuclear exchange to settle East-West differences. As a people we understood the problem better then than we have understood it since. And the reason may be that we have been listening to the experts, who seek to instruct us in the mathematics of nuclear exchange and in the game theories that leave out all human equations.

Of course, if the leaders of the country and the political thinkers can be made to function like machines, then you don't have to talk about the human equation. You just put the problem on a computer, feed your assumptions into it, and there you are! But then the political side, the human equation, all the things that life is really about, are gone.

When Russia invaded Czechoslovakia last summer there was no violent resistance by the Czechs. You might ask whether this was wise or not. In one view the Czech people were "chicken" for not standing up even though the odds were hopeless. But is the survival of a people and their culture not more important than a "heroic" gesture? There can be two answers to that question. But it seems to me that the real question does lie along those lines. All along I have had the feeling that no one in these times, except perhaps the Russians on one or two occasions, has dared to take chances for the survival of the culture.

HERZFELD: I am quite aware that even to contemplate the kind of calculations one must make in matters of military security causes real and valid revulsion in many people, and not just among the young. I must point out, however, that this revulsion is the kind that any nonmedical person feels when he accidentally walks into an operating room while an operation is going on. His reaction is valid, but it does not help him understand the problem of medicine very much.

Personally, I prefer to try to deal in as objective and quantifiable a way as I can with what might be an unlikely and is certainly an undesirable eventuality, thermonuclear war. Obviously such calculations and numerical attempts at understanding must be done well, and the figures must be used honestly. The fact that some people have not always done this is not an argument against trying to understand, with some precision, what some of these numbers are and what they mean.

It is worth recalling that the naval treaties of the 1920's and 1930's involved serious attempts by serious, thoughtful people to limit, with great precision and in great detail, the kinds of warships different countries could build, the limitations on their size, numbers, armament, and displacement. These agreements certainly had one benefit: They kept many countries from spending an awful lot of money on naval armaments between 1920 and 1940.

Technology Versus Democracy

WHEELER: A major issue, it seems to me, is that we are entering into a new era with a new kind of policy-forming and legislative process. We've been in the beginning of that era for some time, ever since the atomic bomb. Now it is taking a more virulent form.

Our traditional legislative and policy-forming institutions were founded on the assumption that men of ordinary wisdom have the capacity, and would always have the capacity, to make rational judgments and to engage in deliberative procedures adequate to the solution of all the problems that might conceivably arise concerning the welfare of our country. But it is now obvious, with the kinds of problems we have been discussing here, that that condition no longer exists. In other words, the information and the understanding needed to come to a reasoned position on an intense, important public issue such as the ABM are held today by a group of people who are not sufficiently involved in the legislative process to insure wise deliberation in the resolution of that issue.

We are coming to the point where true legislative processes are occurring in the realm of science policy rather than in the halls of the legislatures. This is a key problem—how to bring matters that involve complex technology and difficult scientific questions into what might be called the realm of the Constitution. How do you constitutionalize science?

One of the real sadnesses here is that while this issue of the ABM is so terribly important and may indeed shape the outlines of our culture for many years to come, and while there may be intense debate in a very small circle, there is nothing like the spill-out and the resonance on this issue among the people in general that there was in the past at the time of the Teller-Pauling debates on thermonuclear arms, or even with regard to the test-ban treaty.

What we need on this issue is some way of bringing into an institutional framework and into the public arena a counterpart of the Teller-Pauling debates. I would hope we might be able to devise some way of bringing this issue into the normal, traditional, popular, and deliberative channels of the country.

McGovern: I am very grateful for the public discussion we are having of the issue here. One of the shortcomings in our defense decisions has been that often they have been made by the so-called experts without the light of day focused on them. For a good many years I have been more and more skeptical of the decision-making process under which we commit enormous amounts of public money to highly doubtful military gadgets that add nothing to our security. Even some of the loftiest advisers to our defense establishment have over the years demonstrated that they are long on theory and short on common sense, compassion, and a concern for the human interest.

Dr. Rabi made the point well. If we succeed, at long last, in building a theoretically airtight defense structure but in the process create the kind of allocation of resources that neglects our most acute internal, domestic problems, we may discover that we have built a shield around a value system that is no longer worth protecting.

Rabi: What Congress can do is to lay down the national objectives. We have been suffering a great deal from not having a clear discussion of national objectives. We lack goals. As I said, Mr. Eisenhower's objective was the preservation of the American way of life, our culture. That is number one. If this were clearly our goal, it would have an enormous effect on every element of our policy and on the direction in which we are going. Then the search for a balance of terror would not have been the direction we would have taken.

With all respect to the military people, they should not have had the job of setting national objectives, as they very often seem to. After we have a clear understanding and a clear statement of where we want to go, we can discuss with the experts the various ways of achieving that objective on all sides, including the military side.

WHEELER: I agree. The difficulty, of course, in establishing goals is that once the technical and scientific groundwork is set up, the debate occurs within that technical and scientific frame of reference. So if you have goals that do not happen to coincide with the direction and the premises of the technical system, you are not going to be able to do very much about achieving those goals. There is a kind of technological imperative at work here that makes it very difficult for the deliberative political representatives to get a toehold into an extremely complex technical situation and to reassert the primacy of goals and the traditional goal-establishing institutions.

McGOVERN: We got into the Vietnam War largely through administrative decisions rather than Congressional decisions. Congress failed to exercise its foreign policy responsibilities. It wasn't until about 1965 that we had the beginning of a substantive debate in the Senate about our objectives in Vietnam. Until that time decisions about Vietnam were made almost without any Congressional surveillance. I think the same thing has been happening with reference to the ABM. It is just now that we are beginning to generate some public discussion of it in the Congress. I don't mean to imply that there is not enormous Congressional pressure to move ahead on the ABM without careful examination of the matter; it exists, and we all feel it. But I would like to think that our experience in Vietnam has led to an awakening of public opinion and to a reawakening in the Congress, so that a searching discussion of the ABM will now get under way.

HERZFELD: Senator McGovern is correct when he says there has not been much debate in the Congress on the ABM, if one interprets this to mean debate on the floor of either house. But I have been before at least five different Congressional committees to testify about the ABM since the early 1960's. And I have found a remarkable degree of willingness to listen and ability to debate this issue. This is particularly true in the Appropriations Committee.

WIESNER: If you had a secret ballot on the ABM, the Senate would vote against it.

HERZFELD: That may be. But I only wanted to point out that a great deal of genuine, informed deliberation goes on in the various committees concerned with defense.

Crisis Effects from the Arms Race

SCHURMANN: Throughout this discussion we have been talking about the possibility of a nuclear war and whether the ABM would encourage arms escalation. I think we also ought to consider certain other effects of either the ABM or new offensive weaponry like MIRV, effects that may be extremely dangerous because they would create an even more unsettled world situation.

Vietnam may not be the last great international tension we will have to face. In the coming years, even in the coming months, we may be facing in the Middle East another area of extraordinary explosive tension.

My own feeling is that we did have a period, after the Cuban missile crisis, when things were beginning to settle down (with the exception of Vietnam, of course). We did have a partial nuclear test-ban treaty. There was Soviet-American co-operation in Laos. There was a probable indication of Soviet-American co-operation in the Congo. Certainly there was some kind of Soviet-American understanding over Cuba.

There is no doubt that the Soviet Union has the capability (and the will) of abetting, creating, and fostering a whole series of tense situations throughout the world. But what I am suggesting is that the creating of tensions and crisis situations cannot be dissociated from what happens in the nuclear arms race, whether the arms escalation is on the defensive or offensive side. Let me just quote for you an item in this morning's

New York Times. Senators Claiborne Pell and Albert Gore went to visit Premier Kosygin in Moscow, and Mr. Kosygin told the Senators that "the relaxation of tension cannot be achieved if one power amasses a great superiority of military strength."

I don't think it makes much sense to try to blame either the Russians or ourselves for the escalation. We have escalated in Vietnam and in our offensive nuclear weapons. They escalated with ICBM's in 1966. Whether one side calls what the other side does escalation and what it does itself counterescalation is immaterial. Both sides have contributed to the heating up of the arms race.

The point is that escalation of arms leads to escalation in tension and crisis in various parts of the world. The likelihood is not so much that someone will press the button and start a general nuclear war, but that there will be a series of small attacks, little wars, whether in the Israeli-Arab world, Cuba again, or wherever. The danger is that these small attacks can, like Vietnam, grow, and then certain people will again seriously consider the use of tactical nuclear weapons.

Far more is involved here than simply the cost-effectiveness of the ABM, and the differences, errors, and misjudgments that might be found in this scenario or that, and whether or not the numbers used by Secretary McNamara are correct.

My strong feeling is that the ABM and MIRV are an arms escalation that will heat up not only the arms race as such but the world situation in general.

BERLE: Conceivably, if a crisis were rightly handled, one could begin to get some agreement on arms limitation. A Middle East crisis, as you suggest, could come very soon. If it does, I would hope it could be used instead of abused, so that we might try to see if we could not grapple with some of the ghastly realities of our nuclear age. Such a crisis, I repeat, could come quite soon. For that reason it seems to me that the argument about whether twenty million or thirty million lives would be saved by deploying the ABM simply loses its validity. You do not have to destroy a man's entire body to destroy him. If you can put a bullet through his brain, that is all you need to

do. If the nerve centers of a country are destroyed, it is immaterial whether there are "only" five million rather than eighty
million people killed.

One of the reasons I oppose the ABM is that I think we are
indeed moving into the kind of international crisis situation in
which we will not be able to use that defensive system, at least
not in time, and in which our objective ought to be to emerge
from the crisis with the beginnings of an elementary world law.

I might add that it may be precisely because of some of the
technical difficulties and weaknesses in a missile defense system
that we might reach a point where we could begin to emerge
from the balance-of-terror situation that now exists.

SCHURMANN: I think we may be in the beginning of a new
kind of crisis situation, particularly in the Middle East. The
Middle East crisis has been shifting from the old continual
confrontation between the Israelis and Arabs to one between
the United States and the Soviet Union. There has been a
Soviet build-up in the Mediterranean, Soviet searching and
attempted surveillance of Polaris submarines in the Mediterranean. A calm discussion of the ABM and nuclear weapons of
the kind we have been having among ourselves these past two
days may not be possible if we have a new, highly intensified
crisis situation in the Middle East, one that could threaten to
compound.

By definition, a crisis situation can go either of two ways. In
the early Eisenhower period it led to peace in Korea. The Cuban
missile crisis led to a partial test-ban treaty. We know what the
Vietnam decisions early in the Johnson Administration led to.
One can point to pre-World-War-I history and find a series of
crises that were successfully resolved. That is not the point.
Fifteen crises in a row may have been resolved successfully, but
then came July, 1914, and that was the end of it.

I am wondering in what ways a direct Soviet-American confrontation in the Middle East, such as we had over the missile
crisis in Cuba, could be propelled into constructive directions
including, I would imagine, some sort of de-escalating or at

least stabilizing adjustment in the offensive and defensive postures of the two super-powers.

BERLE: After the Korean War had been reduced to a cease-fire, Mr. Eisenhower found it expedient to land Marines in Lebanon. Both actions may have proceeded from the same policy, or perhaps instinct. My own feeling is that when you see that a crisis is imminent, you look for the appropriate moment and then you head into it, not out of it. This means you try to call a conference and proceed from that basis. In this case, the objective would be not a resolution that in any event would be only for the moment, so to speak, but an understanding regarding the whole business of nuclear armament.

That is the *ultima ratio regnum* (the last argument of kings). A crisis may offer the opportunity to go straight for the main problem that all of us have been discussing here. I don't know whether that is possible. But that is my hope. And if, God forbid, I were making the objectives for the next Administration, that would be my objective.

EPILOGUE
Why Not Try the Rule of Law?
William O. Douglas

It is good that this question of missiles and the defense against them is being discussed publicly and being debated. One can hear the H-bomb ticking away as this dialogue goes on.

I am no expert, but my lay judgment is that the manufacture of these systems of missile defense will make the military-industrial complex rich, will result in the production of huge piles of junk, and will be meaningless in terms of survival. Indeed, our preoccupation with problems of this character reveals the growing political bankruptcy of this nation.

My personal judgment is that the salvation of the world lies in a pursuit of a rule of law, not the anti-ballistic missile.

Our best brains have concentrated on many false targets in our dealings with the Russians. The Cold War—a bilateral state of mind arranged by Stalin and by Truman—produced many such targets. We concluded that Russia's determination to control eastern Europe implied a determination to attack

79

and control western Europe. No credible evidence appeared in the ensuing twenty years to support that conclusion. Yet it was on that assumption that West Germany was rearmed, the Cold War frozen, and a nuclear arms race, now picking up new momentum, was launched.

What Russia did to the Baltic states and later to Hungary and Czechoslovakia was shocking. We assume that our Monroe Doctrine makes morally palatable what we did in the Dominican Republic and Nicaragua. Yet we are reluctant to tolerate such policing of their neighbors by other nations.

The ancient game of balance of power becomes more dangerous as the nuclear age develops. The present balance of power is fired by ideological differences that have overtones as fierce as those between Christianity and Islam that once tore the world asunder.

History shows that as one military power marshals its resources for possible use against the opponent, the latter responds. Preparedness becomes a way of life. It is easy to sell, for it fans the sparks of fear in the hearts of people. And so the race is on. History, I think, demonstrates that preparedness is no deterrent to war. The failure of one nation to keep apace of the enemy may, of course, be disastrous. The stories of Carthage versus Rome, and Persia versus Alexander, illustrate the risk faced by Israel if she should ever fall behind. That risk often becomes intolerable, in the absence of a rule of law under which disputes can be settled. Ernest Cuneo, I think, tells the whole story in *Science and History*. The compulsion of nations to balance power only accelerates the acquisition of more power by each side and invariably results in war.

Many think that the pattern has been changed with the advent of nuclear war because a nuclear holocaust is too appalling to contemplate. Yet emotions run deep on both sides of the Cold War; and there are issues that so greatly implicate the vital interests of every nation as to make even the risk of extermination not too heavy a price to pay to preserve those vital interests.

We live indeed in a condition of world anarchy, where an

evangelist of one ideology wages war in Vietnam, and the evangelist of an opposed ideology promotes the waging of war in the Middle East. Each is living dangerously in terms of the risks of nuclear war. Apart from that risk, the waging of war under the modern regime of technology is much, much too expensive for any nation.

Man's choice must lie in other directions if he is to survive. The aim must be the prevention of war. That is to say, the search must be for a regime of the rule of law to settle controversies between nations.

We need, I think, summit conference after summit conference to discuss specific proposals inaugurating a rule of law.

Nations, like the men who compose them, are inherently predatory. Conflicts can never be eliminated. That is why the talk of "peace" that we hear so much about is usually fraudulent talk. The only talk that is constructive is talk about how to design procedures to handle conflicts between nations. When we look ahead, we can say that those conflicts are as certain to develop as the sun is certain to rise.

It is said that agreements of that kind are impossible with Soviet Russia. One who studies post-World-War-II history will find a large degree of intransigence on the part of Russia when it comes to co-operative projects at the world level. Russia's intransigence, however, has been paralleled by our own intransigence, as epitomized by John Foster Dulles. Those two schools of intransigence are indeed oppressively similar, resulting, for example, in the refusal of either nation to submit her international quarrels to the International Court of Justice.

There is a frequently repeated idea that co-operation with an imperialistic Soviet Union is not only distasteful to the American voter but also unsafe for the peace of the world. Yet there can be no rule of law without co-operation, and there can be no real security for mankind without a rule of law.

At bottom, both Russia and the United States are realists; and despite ideological differences the two nations have concluded over forty treaties and executive agreements since 1917. Of these forty, twenty-five are still in force today. Put together into one mosaic, they do not form a regime of law governing all disputes between the two countries. But each treaty or agreement does contain threads of that design, dealing with specific concrete issues.

If we are not to become politically bankrupt in managing the crises of this nuclear age, Russia and the United States *must* hammer out a consensus on the procedures that will peacefully resolve the crucial conflicts between the great powers and between the lesser ones as well.

The list is long, and the selection cannot be made unilaterally. How can we get a consensus on an agenda for the solution of potential conflicts?

We can put aside as non-negotiable the placement of Russian missiles in Cuba or the settlement of crises between Russia and the countries of eastern Europe through American intervention.

Can access to West Berlin be put into the justifiable category and be subject to adjudication by a defined tribunal?

Border and boundary problems have always loomed large. Territorial questions mixed with border problems have plagued Israel. Can the United States and Russia agree on their resolution under a regime of law?

The problems of the territorial seas create numerous friction points, as illustrated this year by the Pueblo incident and last year by the Gulf of Aqaba episode. Can such conflicts between little nations, or between great powers, or between a great power and a lesser power, be channeled into legal tribunals?

No one knows the answers. I suggest, however, that the search be launched in summit meeting after summit meeting. This search will not be complete until the means of getting rid of nuclear weapons altogether is part of the movement for organized peace.

The problem is beset with tremendous difficulties, as we are all plagued with the idea of protecting our own sovereignty. That is as true of the United States as it is of Russia. The protection of sovereignty has all the ingredients of a rabble-rousing slogan. But reason tells us that only by giving up a bit of sovereignty can all the nations move forward. It took the surrender of a considerable slice of sovereignty to get the Postal Union, but it is this Postal Union that makes it possible to send letters to some hundred and thirty nations and to receive letters from people in those nations. It was the Convention on Civil Aviation that made possible an efficient network of air routes over some ninety nations around the globe. So it goes from treaty to treaty. One can often get by surrender of a bit of sovereignty more than he surrenders.

What any people can get in terms of a rule of law would contribute more to their security than what they have stockpiled in the form of nuclear weapons.

Yet even treaties to confine the use of nuclear power are suspect. We hear silly reasons for failure to confirm the nuclear nonproliferation treaty with Russia. Some suggest it should be postponed because somehow or other it is an endorsement of communism. Some think a delay is necessary until we solve the problem of the electromagnetic pulse given off by a nuclear explosion and its impact upon our system of internal communications. Yet subjecting nuclear power to the rule of law is a necessary step toward survival. Not that the nuclear nonproliferation treaty by itself will work magic. But, like the hot line between the White House and the Kremlin, it is one of the building-blocks necessary for the structure known as the rule of law.

The old preoccupations with ideas of national power and supremacy are more than antiquated. Today they conflict with human welfare and human survival. The test that is now relevant for Russians and Americans alike is not how many megatons of obliterative force can be accumulated, but whether the species now confronted with the stark prospect of obliteration can find common ground for survival.

Disarmament alone is not the answer. For as I said, man is inherently predatory, and a rule of law is as necessary to control nations as it is to control individuals. The world anarchy we face makes the problem extremely difficult. But the ticking of the H-bomb should make us hurry to escape the paralysis of the political bankruptcy that seems to have overtaken us.

The only known alternative to the rule of force is the rule of law. The search for a rule of law adequate for world survival, not the missile race, should preoccupy us. A world that will not admit the Peking regime to its councils (a regime representing one fourth of the people of the world) is a world that needs awakening. I assure you that lawyers and jurists across the globe can make the rule of law a fresh reality once the politicians begin to listen.

Appendixes

Appendix I

The ABM Decision, Viewed by Adolf A. Berle, Neil H. Jacoby, Charles M. Herzfeld, Freeman Dyson

ADOLF A. BERLE

I oppose the proposed construction and deployment of the anti-ballistic-missile system. My reasons for opposing further development of such a system differ from many of the arguments presented.

I am not in favor of unilateral disarmament. I believe disarmament agreements, beginning with the Soviet Union, can and will eventually be concluded. We have not yet arrived at a *détente* with the Soviet Union, although I think we must and will have one within a few years. The missile crisis with Cuba in 1961–62, the Tri-Continental Congress of Havana in 1964, the Czechoslovakian invasion of 1968, and the current Soviet armament build-up in Egypt and the Mediterranean all indicate that proclamations of an end to the Cold War were, to put it mildly, premature. One may yet anticipate its end, but the prospect of imminent events could test that hope in international crises more dangerous than those traversed since the end of World War II. Military power will be a regrettable but necessary factor in helping us to solve them peacefully.

Embarking nevertheless on a vast program of competitive anti-ballistic-missile defense at this time seems to offer little if any real defense or safety for our population and provides a good excuse for a further plunge into an unlimited arms race. Its only certain result is that an immense sum of money, now estimated at fifty billion dollars, will be spent, diverting a corresponding amount of technical and economic effort from constructive endeavor into sterile work.

The ABM movement is not, I think, principally the result of corrupt military-industrial lobbying in Washington. Construction and deployment of such a system undoubtedly would temporarily benefit a number of electronic and munitions corporations and would enhance the importance of some Pentagon units. We all remember President Eisenhower's warning against the power of the military-industrial complex. We have all heard unproved accusations that the United States is being decoyed into vast, expensive, sterile, and dangerous enterprises by self-interested lobbying and political activities carried on by American companies seeking profit from the armament supply business. I myself am not persuaded that the current push is caused by such activities, although I concede there may have been some.

The ABM proposal can, I think, be debated on its merits without being ascribed to lobbying or corrupt promotion. On those merits, however, the ABM plunge seems impossible to justify. No expert is prepared to state that the ABM or any foreseeable evolution of it can safeguard the United States from the results of nuclear attack. Safeguard apparently can be produced, if at all, only by deterrence, the so-called second strike, which we already have.

At best, fully developed anti-ballistic defense might, in case of attack, save some millions of lives against a total of many tens of millions dead. But the objective of nuclear war is not slaughter of the entire population of the enemy country. Aside from crippling its second-strike capacity, destruction of the enemy's social, economic, and governmental structure is the nuclear target. No evidence remotely suggests that any ABM system offers enough protection from slaughter and physical destruction that the governmental, social, and economic structure of either the United States or the Soviet Union could survive. If that is true, a fifty-billion-dollar expenditure for its proposed development becomes a sheer waste of money and resources for the United States, or for the Soviet Union if it undertakes similar deployment. Worse yet, it might hinder the possibility of a true agreement with the Soviet Union on nuclear arms limitation, if not on nuclear disarmament. I have no guide to Soviet intentions, still less to their modes of reasoning. But, clearly, a step of this magnitude and gravity is not conducive to agreement; it could, indeed, lead to a Soviet conclusion that no significant agreement could be reached.

Economically the United States has the capacity, I am sure, to commit and spend $50 billion for armament over the next three or four years. It could do this even while it also committed and expended a comparable sum for its cities, its education, and its poor. The American Gross National Product for 1968 will be in the vicinity of $800 billion at the very least for 1969, with a probability of its reaching $910 billion. It is economically manageable to channel enough of the increase into armament or into social reconstruction or even into both at once through a considered four- or five-year plan. But the capacity to do this is no argument whatsoever for unnecessary expenditure. The simple fact is that the results of an anti-ballistic-missile campaign are not worth the expense. If expenditures of this magnitude are to be considered, they ought to be directed, first, toward those activities likely to reduce the danger of war, and second, toward an increase in the tensile strength of the American social system. This conference is neither the time nor the place to suggest such a plan of expenditure, although I think I could do so. I merely wish to say that anti-ballistic-missile spending on this scale seems indefensible when its sole short-term effect will be the creation of a relatively useless system and its probably far-reaching military effect will be to propel the Soviet Union and the United States into a new, more dangerous, and infinitely more wasteful stretch in the armament race.

NEIL H. JACOBY

Some opponents of the ABM contend that the decision to deploy a light system reflected the pressures of the military-industrial complex, moved by motives of politics and profit, and did not represent an honest evaluation of technical, economic, and military factors. Ever since President Eisenhower warned against the danger of an alliance between the weapon-hungry armed services and profit-seeking defense companies in his Farewell Message of 1960, the notion has persisted that military procurement decisions are dominated by private rather than national interests.

This view does not withstand objective analysis. There is no evidence that defense firms control military expenditures or that they are in league with the Pentagon to inflate the defense budget. Indeed, all the evidence runs to the contrary. The federal Executive has repeatedly canceled large military procurement programs that caused severe distress to defense firms and the communities in which they operated. Examples include the precipitous drops in military procurement after World War II and the Korean War, the cancellation of the B-70 manned bomber program in 1959, the termination of the Nike-Zeus ABM project in 1962, and the recent cutbacks in the military and civilian space programs. If the military-industrial complex really dominated defense spending decisions, surely it would have been able to prevent the painful industrial adjustments it has endured.

It should be recalled that more often than not Congress has expanded appropriations for military procurement beyond the levels recommended by the President and the Department of Defense. It cannot be argued that this reflects the influence of the military-industrial complex. There are far more Congressmen who represent districts in which nondefense industries would benefit from civilian uses of federal funds released from armaments than there are districts in which defense industries dominate the local economy. It is illogical to attribute over-weening power over national security policies to a large and heterogeneous group of business corporations that collectively account for under three and a half per cent of the G.N.P.—less than $30 billion of military procurement in a national product of $850 billion a year. Military procurement contracts carry notoriously low margins of profit. All large aerospace companies have sought to diversify into civilian products in order to in-crease and stabilize their earning power and the market value of their stocks.

Of course, the military services do press hard for more weap-onry. Defense corporations are aggressive salesmen of their products. Yet, as J. Raymond has pointed out, the openness of the annual debate on the defense budget, the wide divergence of opinion both among the generals and between them and the Executive and Congress, and the great geographic inequalities of the economic benefits from defense spending combine to guard against undue influence by private or local interests. Whether right or wrong, the ABM decision undoubtedly re-flected a search for the national interest.

The Cost-Exchange Ratio Between Defense and Offense

The decision to spend five billion dollars on an ABM system can be examined on economic grounds. Economists usually evaluate proposals for new public programs by the process of cost-benefit analysis. This is a technique for calculating the benefits to be derived from spending a given amount of money in each of several alternative ways to attain a specified purpose. Thus one may discover how to maximize benefits at a given cost or to minimize the cost of obtaining a specified benefit. In the Pentagon this technique is known as cost-effectiveness analysis, probably because it puts language under serious strain to refer to the death of a hundred million Russians or the destruction of a hundred billion dollars of Soviet capital as a benefit.

When one examines the decision to spend five billion dollars on an ABM system, he must compare its effectiveness with that of alternative measures for purchasing the same amount of national security with an outlay of five billion dollars, such as buying additional ICBM's or increasing the power of present ICBM's to penetrate enemy defenses. He comes up against the problem of measuring the cost-exchange ratio. This is the ratio of the amount of defense outlays required to reduce by a specified amount the damage suffered from an enemy attack to the amount of offense outlays required to offset or cancel the reduction in damage. Until recent years nuclear weapons technology strongly favored offense, and the cost-exchange ratio was substantially greater than one-to-one. Recent progress in technology, however, such as radars, guidance systems, and fast-acceleration rockets, appears to have raised the cost-effectiveness of defense to the point where the cost-exchange ratio is close to unity for the middle range of survival percentages. (This ratio will be smaller for high-survival percentages and larger for medium-survival levels because the offense always has the option of concentrating his attack on points unknown in advance to the defense.) A given expenditure on strategic forces can either increase the damage one side inflicts on the other or reduce the damage the other side inflicts upon it by about the same amount. Thus a given outlay will have the same effect upon the nuclear balance whether it is spent on ICBM or ABM systems. Granting these premises, the United States buys as much national security by spending five billion dollars on the Sentinel system as by spending it on offensive weapons.

Transferability of ABM Resources

Opponents contend that deployment of the Sentinel system will have small value for the nation in comparison with the values sacrificed by not spending the money on civilian programs, such as education, transportation, urban renewal, or public assistance. They say its opportunity costs are large.

This argument assumes, first, that funds are the effective constraint upon actions to resolve social problems, and second, that the real resources used in developing and producing missile defenses are highly transferable to and from civilian uses. Both assumptions are of dubious merit.

There is a growing appreciation that fresh ideas and a new public will, rather than more money, are the critical elements needed to resolve urban and social difficulties. In a nation whose federal government revenues expand twelve billion dollars a year as a result of economic growth, financial resources are not the real constraint. Furthermore, the real resources released by canceling the Sentinel program could not readily be re-employed productively in civilian undertakings. Nor could these resources be quickly mobilized to produce an ABM defense in the event that world developments made such a decision imperative later on. Transferability is limited.

The real resources needed in missile defense are highly specialized teams of scientists, engineers, and technologists, skilled in electronics, nucleonics, metallurgy, and allied sciences. Years are required to acquire these abilities, and more years are needed to create effective working organizations of such specialists. These organizations cannot be used effectively in civilian tasks, except perhaps in the space program. Over a period of five to ten years, the opportunity costs of employing these resources in an ABM program are, therefore, not high from a social point of view. Of course, the opportunity costs become large if one assumes that an ABM system will never be needed, an heroic assumption in the present state of the world.

Let us consider the other side of the matter, the transferability of specialized resources into ABM work. If the light ABM program is abandoned now, will there be time available to reconstruct specialized research, development, and production organizations should the national interest clearly require them in the future? After several years of stagnation, can U.S. capabilities in missile defense technology be developed soon enough? Cannot a limited ABM investment now be considered as an insurance premium against the contingencies of heavy ABM build-ups by the communist powers or future technological developments that strongly favor defense? No doubt these were among the considerations that moved former Secretary of Defense McNamara to support the limited ABM system.

In reaching a judgment on this matter, the relatively small scale of the light ABM program should be remembered. When spread over several years, the annual capital and maintenance costs would add something like two per cent to the eighty-three-billion-dollar annual defense budget. They would be considerably smaller than the annual cost to our citizens of farm subsidies or petroleum import quotas. We may note, in passing, that the national security values of the ABM system would not have to exceed zero in order to surpass those of such civilian expenditures.

In summary, building the Sentinel system does not require the American people to defer important civilian tasks. Viewed over a period of five or ten years, its opportunity costs are comparatively small. On the other hand, the military risks of deferring an ABM defense are not negligible, considering the long lead-time necessary for research, development, production, and deployment.

In Conclusion

A brief assessment of issues in the ABM debate does not lead to a clear conclusion that one may hold with high confidence. There are too many large uncertainties attached to the underlying data. The variables are too heterogeneous to be weighed and evaluated upon a common scale. In the end the decision on the Sentinel system must rest more on judgment than on analysis.

The arguments we have examined are of very unequal weight, and each analyst of the ABM problem will have his own system of weights. To this observer, the political consequences of deploying Sentinel are of dominant importance. If they were adverse, even powerful technological, military, and economic reasons for building an ABM defense would not justify it. However, a light missile-defense of the United States can be supported because it can possibly improve the chances for arms limitation and ultimate disarmament; at the worst, it will not diminish those chances.

At the minimum, the decision to deploy the Sentinel system was not manifestly unwise. This observer would state the conclusion affirmatively: The balance of considerations favors the beginning of a limited missile-defense effort at this time.

CHARLES M. HERZFELD

I would like to summarize the arguments about two limiting cases, one, the thin area-defense, such as Sentinel, the other, the thick city-defense. The thin system is no help in confrontation with a sophisticated attack, and the thick system is not much help. The thin system is quite effective against an unsophisticated attack; the thick system is more effective than is necessary. Both systems provide marginal, though possibly important, advantages in times of serious crisis, accident, and so forth. Both systems provide firebreaks in very serious crises, because they make small token attacks initiated for bargaining purposes ineffective and not credible. Finally, the thin system is much less likely than the thick system to exacerbate the arms race with the Soviet Union or to induce miscalculations in the United States or the Soviet Union concerning its effectiveness.

It is my conviction that a thick defense buys too little for the probable cost and would exacerbate the arms race with the Soviet Union. A thick system also could mislead a future U.S. leadership into thinking that the defense system was really better than was supposed, and hence encourage more risk-taking than is desirable. On the other hand, a thin system would provide the important secondary benefits mentioned above without inducing the undesirable effects just mentioned. I believe, however, that a decision to deploy an ABM system is not really a compelling decision (like the decision to deploy ICBM's, for which there really was no sensible alternative) but is in some important senses a fragile decision. The decision could be reversed or modified by a large number of things that could happen.

It is perhaps of interest to summarize for the record the sheer magnitude of the U.S. research and development effort in this area, which has been carried on over the last five to ten years. The grand total of research and development expended on the ABM so far is approximately four billion dollars. This includes about ten years of Nike-X and Nike-Zeus funding, and about nine years of Project Defender effort. This is a larger and more thorough research and development effort than has been expended on any other single military problem. The magnitude of the U.S. effort on penetration is comparable. A fair fraction of the research and development on U.S. offensive forces has led to better penetration capability, particularly to the new systems of Minuteman III and Poseidon. Also, a large fraction of the information obtained from ABM research and development has been directly applicable to improving penetration capability.

These costs have gone to support relevant laboratory work and very extensive flight programs and field measurement programs, as well as radar and missile development. Also a comparatively very large effort has gone into detailed system studies. It is hard for the outsider to imagine how detailed these system studies were, and how many of them were carried out (indeed still are carried out). The total effort has been large. More importantly, the effort has been of very high quality. The best technical talent of universities, of industry, and of the government were devoted to this effort.

The magnitude of the effort on the ABM and penetration is important in several ways. First of all, and most significantly, the detailed understanding of the ABM and penetration problem in the United States *assures* the ability of the United States to penetrate any likely defense, and hence protects and keeps credible our deterrent. Second, this deep understanding indicates that it is very unlikely that one could get equivalent knowledge for a much smaller effort. Hence it is highly unlikely that a Sentinel-type system will be made obsolete by any less sophisticated nation either quickly or cheaply. This serves to produce perhaps a mild measure of stability for at least a few years in the otherwise rapidly evolving stretegic situation.

Freeman Dyson

It is obvious that a defense system will not save everyone's life in the event of a nuclear war. That is not the aim of the enterprise, although occasionally there have been claims of that sort made. What a defense system will do is save those targets that are not attacked.

In the paper wars that are constantly being fought in the community of scholars, analyzing offense and defense, the offense tends to be conservative. The reason is that you have a very strong desire to maintain what is called an assured-destruction capability. Therefore, you plan to attack targets giving the defense considerable benefit of various doubts. It generally turns out that if you attack a target at all, you expect to kill it with something like ninety-five per cent probability. If you cannot be sure of killing a target with ninety-five per cent probability, then it is better not to attack it. This is what one calls the assured-destruction capability.

Now, of course, those targets that are not attacked are not destroyed. The consequence of this is that the defense actually works independently of whether it does well in the technical sense. It may in fact do very well, or it may fail miserably; a target that is attacked with twenty-five missiles may get hit by twenty-five missiles, in which case the defense has failed miserably; or it may get hit by two missiles, in which case the defense has done well. In both cases, the target is destroyed. But twenty-four other cities are not attacked because of the concentration on this one target.

But if a system is deployed that has a reasonable chance of

being technically effective, it is a militarily effective system. It may be technically true that penetration is easy—I'm not even sure of that—but it is certainly very hard to feel confident enough of this to build the assumption into the structure of an offensive force. If you are sitting in a city that is not attacked, the defense has worked as far as you are concerned, even if you did not solve the decoy discrimination problem.

My second point is that the Sentinel system is a rather better defense for missile forces than it is for cities. This has been more or less admitted by former Secretary McNamara, who said in announcing the deployment that it was intended as a defense of cities against Chinese attack and as a partial defense of the missile force against a Soviet attack. A defense against a Soviet attack is a much more serious proposition than one directed against a Chinese attack. Sentinel defends Minutemen better than cities because the meaning of defense is quite different in the two cases.

In trying to defend cities, there is no choice of what to defend—cities are there, places where large populations are concentrated. It is quite otherwise with military targets. In the case of the Minuteman force, there are a thousand targets. A good defense would be one in which, say, five hundred of those survived, and it does not matter which five hundred. Concentrating defenses on particular places, a wide margin of uncertainty in the total effectiveness can be allowed and there would still be a good defense of your military force.

There is a particular reason for taking seriously the need for a defense of the missile forces in the next five or ten years because of the new technical development of the MIRV, one missile carrying a substantial number of independently guided warheads that can attack separate targets. If one missile launcher could destroy, say, three or four of the opponent's launchers, then he cannot be sure he has an effective deterrent. There is an incentive for a first strike, since a land-based missile force would be liable to be wiped out even by a numerically inferior force on the other side.

I believe that the danger involved in this MIRV development has not been stressed sufficiently in the public statements that have been made. I consider it the most dangerous thing that is coming up. I believe that if MIRV is put into operation, and if the guidance accuracy is improved, as people generally assume it will be, then we will be driven to active defense of the missile force as the only means of assuring stability. I consider the Sentinel system a first step in that direction.

I protest the tendency for opponents of defense systems to talk as though deterrence, that is, an assured-destruction capability, were inconsistent with building a strong active defense. I think the two things are quite consistent and can be carried through in a balanced fashion. In the long run, nobody expects the defense to be so good that it will eliminate the catastrophic aspects of a nuclear war. The most we can expect is to hold down the consequences so that some tens of millions, not hundreds of millions, of people would be killed on each side. The question is whether that is sufficient for what is called deterrence. I would say unquestionably that it is; I myself would be quite adequately deterred by the thought that twenty million people in my own country would be killed if I started a war.

What the active defense will do, if its future is as bright as I think it is, is make it extremely difficult to destroy a country permanently—that is, to put a country out of business for a hundred or two hundred years, to reduce its inhabitants to complete barbarism and disorganization.

The economics of attack and defense tends to have this character: The relative cost of defense is extremely high if you try to defend ninety-five per cent of your people; it is moderate if you try to defend seventy-five per cent; and it becomes quite low if you try to defend twenty-five per cent. If the defense is prepared to spend, roughly speaking, up to the point where the cost-exchange ratio swings over to being favorable to the offense, then you will arrive at some sort of equilibrium between offense and defense, at a level where if you are not saving ninety-five per cent of the people, at least you are not losing seventy-five per cent of them.

I consider this not an undesirable situation. Each side will have the capability of destroying a substantial number of people, but not such a huge number as would constitute some sort of permanent, final solution of its foreign policy problem. In the long run, this is a more stable situation to aim for than the situation we are living in at the moment, in which both sides are almost completely vulnerable.

The question of ethics or morality is not entirely separable from these technical and military questions. If you have the choice, other things being equal, I think you should put money into defense rather than into offense. For some reason this is generally considered to be a hawkish point of view, but I don't believe it is. Fundamentally, I believe it is moral and reasonable to go in for defense to a much greater extent than we have been doing. This has been the historic policy of the Soviet Union. We have always had difficulty in discussing missile defense with Soviet experts because they have the obstinate idea that missile defense is a "good show," while our experts mostly have the view that it is a "bad show."

I believe that the long-term prospects for coming to an informal or even formal stabilization of the arms race are much better if both we and the Soviet Union have a preponderantly defensive orientation. I think Soviet sensitivity to the moral aspects of defense has to do with the fact that they have a more direct knowledge than we have of what it means to have ten million people killed, and they have a less abstract approach to the problem of defense and deterrence.

I would be only too happy if the United States adopted rather more of this philosophy—that is, if we have the choice, we build weapons that can explode only over our own territory. For example, I cannot feel at all sympathetic with those who contemplate using our offense to take out the Chinese nuclear force in China. I would much prefer a system that would take it out over here.

I think this choice between offense and defense is a real issue that our country has to face. In World War II we had to use weapons that were quite inappropriate to the task for which the war was being fought, just because those were the weapons we had. The strategic bombing campaign in Europe, in which I was myself involved, was a largely misguided and wasted effort as far as the prosecution of the war against Germany was concerned. The reason it was done that way was primarily because we had this large bomber force, and all we could do was bomb. It would have been unquestionably much more valuable to us militarily if the production effort had gone into ships rather than bombers—probably permitting us to end the war a year sooner. The same kind of situation can arise in a thermonuclear war; regardless of good intentions, you will be forced to use whatever weapons you have. Even if our offensive forces are designed in the most careful and rational way to give the maximum probability of successful deterrence, I would be much happier with a higher proportion of defensive deployment.

Appendix II

U.S. and Soviet Strategic Ballistic Weaponry

INTERCONTINENTAL BALLISTIC MISSILES
(MT=megatons)

U.S.A.	U.S.S.R.
1,054 ICBM's, including: *	900 ICBM's, including: *
650 Minuteman I, three-stage, solid fuel, 1 MT.	Savage, a three-stage, solid-propellant missile like our Minuteman.
350 Minuteman II, three-stage, solid fuel, 1 MT.	Scrooge, a solid-propellant missile.
54 Titan II, liquid fuel, 5–18 MT.	Sasin, a two-stage, liquid-propellant rocket.
Minuteman III, MIRV-equipped, in production.	

* Source: Secretary of Defense Clark M. Clifford, Defense Posture Report, Fiscal Year 1970.

Source for all tables in Appendix II: "The Military Balance 1968–1969," published by The Institute for Strategic Studies, 18 Adam Street, London W.C. 2, England.

INTERMEDIATE RANGE (IRBM)—MEDIUM RANGE BALLISTIC
MISSILES (MRBM)

U.S.A.	U.S.S.R.
Offensive strategy requires none.	750 of various models deployed to cover western Europe and Japan, including:
	Sandal (MRBM), liquid fuel. Range, 1,100 miles.
	Skean (IRBM), liquid fuel. Range, 2,000 miles.
	Scamp, first shown in Moscow in May, 1965, appears to be completely mobile.

SUBMARINE-LAUNCHED MISSILES (SLM)
(MT=megatons)

U.S.A.	U.S.S.R.
SLM-capable submarines: 41 nuclear-powered, Polaris-fitted; SLM capacity, 16 per submarine.	*SLM-capable submarines:* 30 conventional; SLM capacity, 3 per submarine.
208 Polaris A-2 (0.7 MT), 1,500-mile range.	13 nuclear-powered; SLM capacity, 3 per submarine.
448 Polaris A-3 (0.7 MT), 2,500-mile range.	"Polaris type"; SLM capacity, 16 per submarine; now entering service at rate of 1–2 per year.
Poseidon in production (1.5 MT), MIRV-equipped to replace (A-2) missiles.	149 Serb submarine-launched ballistic missiles (1 MT).
	98 Sark submarine-launched Cruise missiles (0.5 MT).

Anti-Ballistic Missiles (ABM)

U.S.A.	U.S.S.R.
Nike-X: Under development since 1965.	Galosh: Limited ballistic-missile area defense being deployed only around Moscow. Range, 2–300 miles.
Sentinel: Light system announced September 18, 1967.	
Ballistic-missile area and ICBM defense, employing Sprint (short-range) and Spartan (long-range) missiles. Completed development expected by 1972.	

Strategic Bombers

U.S.A.	Payload (lbs.)	U.S.S.R.	Payload (lbs.)
560 B-52's	75,000	110 Bison's (M-4)	20,000
40 B-58's	12,000	100 Bear's (TU-95)	40,000
210 FB-111A's,		750 Badger's (TU-16)	20,000
due 1969–1971		750 Blinder's (TU-22)	12,000

Appendix III

The Sentinel Anti-Ballistic-Missile System

The Sentinel ABM system is not a single weapon, but a co-ordi-
nated array of missiles, radars, and computers. It is composed of
two types of missiles and two types of radars responding and
feeding impulses to a computerized central nervous system. The
first type of radar is a Perimeter Acquisition Radar (PAR),
which is a long-range detection and tracking radar whose beam
can be moved from one direction in the sky to another in a few
millionths of a second so that it can virtually scan the horizon
instantly.

The other radar is a Missile Site Radar (MSR), designed to
track incoming targets at shorter ranges than the PAR and to
track U.S. missiles to their encounter with the attacking missile.

The two missile types are the Spartan and Sprint weapons.
The Spartan, an advanced Zeus missile, is a three-stage rocket,
uses a solid propellant, has a range of several hundred miles,
and is launched from an underground silo. It carries a nuclear

warhead and is designed for instant interception of missiles above the atmosphere. The Sprint is smaller and designed to mop up the work the Spartan does not handle. It is also nuclear-tipped, has two stages, uses solid propellant, and is fired from an underground silo. It will primarily defend strategic targets such as Minuteman Intercontinental Ballistic Missile (ICBM) silos or radars. Because of its limited range and high speed it will act as a last-ditch defense to intercept attacking missiles that have pierced the earlier long-range Spartan umbrella.

As envisioned, the Sentinel system would begin to function when incoming missiles were spotted by the long-range radar (PAR) over a thousand miles away. The PAR would track missiles for a minute or two to establish their trajectory and feed the data to a computer. A Spartan missile would then be triggered to intercept the enemy missiles at a computer-determined point hundreds of miles in outer space. The Spartan would fly at about five thousand miles an hour and at its nearest point to the enemy rocket would explode its hydrogen warhead with the impact of millions of tons of TNT. Although the missiles would not collide, the H-blast of the Spartan would destroy its targets in a wide swath in the vacuum of outer space. Any enemy weapons penetrating this nuclear shield would encounter the short-range Sprint, deployed upon radar warning that missiles were approaching. The Sprint would employ the same procedure as the Spartan to destroy its targets, but its warhead would be smaller and the contact and explosion would be within the atmosphere, about twenty miles in the air.

According to plans, about six PAR radars would be installed along the northern U.S. border and in Hawaii and Alaska. Each would require a 297-acre site and be housed in a concrete building 330 feet wide and 140 feet high. According to published data, the MSR radars and the Spartan sites would need 282-acre plots. Surveys for about 20 Spartan and Sprint sites are underway near Boston, New York, Detroit, Albany (Ga.), Dallas, Salt Lake City, Seattle, San Francisco, Los Angeles, Sedalia (Mo.) and in North Dakota, Wyoming, Montana, and Hawaii. The Spartan sites would be expected to shield the entire country, while the Sprints would be deployed around key sites to assure the survival of retaliatory offensive U.S. missiles and to protect the PAR's.

The cost of this thin system aimed against Chinese attack was originally set at $3.5 billion in early 1967. By the time former Defense Secretary Robert S. McNamara announced the deployment in September, 1967, the cost estimates had risen to $5 billion, and most recent price tags amount to $5.5 billion.

A *Limited-Purpose System.* The Sentinel system is designed to prevent accidental, small, or relatively unsophisticated attacks, such as could be launched by Communist China, from reaching their U.S. targets. It would not be effective against more sophisticated and elusive attacks using rockets with multiple warheads, radar interference devices, low-trajectory missiles that elude the radar, attacks from submarines, or orbital missiles. Massive attacks that Soviet Russia might launch would overwhelm the Spartans and Sprints.

Appendix IV

The McNamara Decision to Deploy the ABM

Defense Secretary Robert S. McNamara gave his formal approval for the production and deployment of a thin Nike-X anti-ballistic-missile system after approximately eight years of debate over the issue, primarily because of the impending threat of a Chinese Communist ICBM capability. In announcing his decision at a meeting of the United Press International Editors and Publishers in San Francisco, Mr. McNamara detailed his continued opposition to the deployment of a more advanced anti-Soviet system. Pertinent excerpts are printed below.

Let me come to the issue that has received so much attention recently: the question of whether or not we should deploy an ABM (anti-ballistic-missile) system against the Soviet nuclear threat. . . .

While we have substantially improved our technology in the field, it is important to understand that none of the systems at the present or foreseeable state of the art would provide an impenetrable shield over the U.S. Were such a shield possible, we would certainly want it—and we would certainly build it. . . .

But what many commentators on this issue overlook is that any such system can rather obviously be defeated by an enemy simply sending more offensive warheads, or dummy warheads, than there are defensive missiles capable of disposing of them. . . .

Were we to deploy a heavy ABM system throughout the U.S., the Soviets would clearly be strongly motivated to so increase their offensive capability as to cancel out our defensive advantage.

. . . We have already initiated offensive weapons programs costing several billions in order to offset the small present Soviet ABM deployment and the possibly more extensive future Soviet ABM deployments. . . .

Now, as I have emphasized, we have already taken the necessary steps to guarantee that our offensive strategic weapons will be able to penetrate future, more advanced, Soviet defenses.

Keeping in mind the careful clockwork of lead time, we will be forced to continue that effort over the next few years if the evidence is that the Soviets intend to turn what is now a light and modest ABM deployment into a massive one. . . .

One of the other uses of an ABM system which we should seriously consider is the greater protection of our strategic offensive forces.

Another is in relation to the emerging nuclear capability of Communist China.

There is evidence that the Chinese are devoting very substantial resources to the development of both nuclear warheads and missile delivery systems. As I stated last January, indications are that they will have medium-range ballistic missiles within a year or so, an initial intercontinental ballistic missile capability in the early 1970's, and a modest force in the mid-seventies.

Up to now, the lead-time factor has allowed us to postpone a decision on whether or not a light ABM deployment might be advantageous as a countermeasure to Communist China's nuclear development.

But the time will shortly be right for us to initiate production if we desire such a system. . . .

We deplore her [China's] development of these weapons, just as we deplore it in other countries. We oppose nuclear proliferation because we believe that in the end it only increases the risk of a common and cataclysmic holocaust. . . .

It would be insane and suicidal for her to so, but one can conceive conditions under which China might miscalculate. We wish to reduce such possibilities to a minimum.

And since, as I have noted, our strategic planning must always be conservative and take into consideration even the possible irrational behavior of potential adversaries, there are marginal grounds for concluding that a light deployment of U.S. ABM's against this possibility is prudent.

The system would be relatively inexpensive—preliminary estimates place the cost at about five billion dollars—and would have a much higher degree of reliability against a Chinese attack than the much more massive and complicated system that some have recommended against a possible Soviet attack.

Moreover, such an ABM deployment designed against a possible Chinese attack would have a number of other advantages. It would provide an additional indication to Asians that we intend to deter China from nuclear blackmail, and thus would contribute toward our goal of discouraging nuclear weapon proliferation among the present non-nuclear countries.

Further, the Chinese-oriented ABM deployment would enable us to add—as a concurrent benefit—a further defense of our Minuteman sites against Soviet attack, which means that at modest cost we would in fact be adding even greater effectiveness to our offensive missile force and avoiding a much more costly expansion of that force.

Finally, such a reasonably reliable ABM system would add protection of our population against the improbable, but possible, accidental launch of an intercontinental missile by any one of the nuclear powers.

After a detailed review of all these considerations, we have decided to go forward with this Chinese-oriented ABM deployment, and we will begin actual production of such a system at the end of this year.

In reaching this decision, I want to emphasize that it contains two possible dangers—and we should guard carefully against each.

The first danger is that we may psychologically lapse into the old oversimplification about the adequacy of nuclear power. The simple truth is that nuclear weapons can serve to deter only a narrow range of threats. This ABM deployment will strengthen our defensive posture—and will enhance the effectiveness of our land-based ICBM offensive forces. But the independent nations of Asia must realize that these benefits are no substitute for their maintaining and, where necessary, strengthening their own conventional forces in order to deal with the more likely threats to the security of the region.

The second danger is also psychological. There is a kind of mad momentum intrinsic to the development of all new nuclear weaponry. If a weapon system works—and works well—there is strong pressure from many directions to procure and deploy the weapon out of all proportion to the prudent level required. . . .

Appendix V

Chronology: Evolution of American ABM Capability and the Debate

The debate over construction of an anti-ballistic-missile system traces back to World War II and the introduction of the German V-2 rockets. Waged between the military and its supporters on one side and Congressional liberals and some scientists on the other, it grew in intensity with the Russian development in 1958 of intercontinental ballistic missiles (ICBM's). The United States' first ICBM, the Atlas, was developed in 1959, followed by the Titan and Minuteman.

Beginning with President Eisenhower in 1960, requests to build and deploy ABM systems were rejected by President Kennedy and President Johnson until the decision was reached in September, 1967, to deploy the light Sentinel system. Nevertheless, the United States from 1954 to 1968 spent about $3 billion on research and development for such a system, and in 1967 an estimated 15,000 military and civilian persons were working on this effort.

The following dateline chronology presents the evolution of the United States development of an ABM capability, beginning in 1955 and including the Nike-Zeus, Nike-X, and the present Sentinel system.

1955

February: United States Department of Defense contracted feasibility studies for proposed Nike-Zeus ABM system with Bell Telephone laboratories.

July: Research and development focused on the intercontinental ballistic missile (ICBM) as the primary target of any emergent ABM system.

1957

January: Full system deployment of the Nike-Zeus ABM system was ordered by the Army.

September: The Atomic Energy Commission completed a feasibility study of the Nike-Zeus missile warhead.

1959

President Eisenhower ordered cessation of Nike-Zeus deployment (radar ineffective, easily overwhelmed by decoys) but authorized continuation of research and development.

June: Joint AEC-Army activities commenced on development engineering for a Zeus missile warhead.

August: First Zeus missile was fired at the White Sands Missile Range.

1960

Soviet Galosh ABM missile was first deployed around Moscow, according to statements made by Soviet leaders in the mid-1960's.

1962

The first successful ICBM-Zeus missile-intercept test was conducted at Kwajalein in the western Pacific.

1962 and 1963

Nike-Zeus successfully intercepted 10 of 14 ICBM's fired from Vandenberg Air Force Base in California.

1963

January 5: Department of Defense authorized the Army to begin research and development on the Nike-X ABM system.

March: Contract for the Sprint missile—short-range, rapid-acceleration component of Nike-X—was awarded to the Martin Company.

The Senate Armed Services Committee, in the first of a series of Congressional attempts to force Executive decisions for the deployment of an ABM system, sought the addition of $196 million for ABM deployment to the defense authorization bill for fiscal 1964. The full Senate, however, rejected the move at the insistence of the administration.

The Soviet Union announced that it had produced a prototype of an effective anti-missile missile.

The Nuclear Test-Ban Treaty was signed during the year.

1964

January: President Johnson ordered cutbacks in U.S. manufacture of fissionable materials and manufacture of arms, and urged the U.S.S.R. to do likewise as a step toward "eventual abolition of arms."

July: Testing of the new MAR (multiple-array radar) system, a radically improved radar designed for Nike-X, was initiated at the White Sands Missile Range.

October: Communist China detonated a low-yield fissionable device, that nation's first atomic bomb.

1965

May: Communist China detonated its second fissionable device, one of low–intermediate yield.

October: The Nike-X deployment study was completed

by the Army and presented to the Secretary of Defense.
November 17: The first successful flight was conducted
of the maneuverable Sprint missile, short-range Nike-X
component.

1966

Development continued on warheads for both the
Sprint and Spartan missiles of the Nike-X system.
May: China detonated its first thermonuclear device
(hydrogen explosion).
October: China tested its first missile-delivered device,
equipped with a low-yield fissionable warhead.
December: China detonated its second thermonuclear
device.

Congress approved $167.9 million for ABM procure-
ment without the request of the Secretary of Defense.
November: Secretary McNamara announced that the
Soviet Union had begun deployment of the Galosh
ABM defense system around Moscow.

1967

January: President Johnson declared that no United
States ABM deployment would be made until comple-
tion of arms control negotiations with the Soviet Union,
and requested Soviet discussions for control of anti-ballistic missiles.

Defense Secretary McNamara, in his defense position
report, presented a detailed argument against deployment of a complete, Russian-oriented ABM system.

General Wheeler, Chairman of the Joint Chiefs of
Staff, expressed disagreement with the McNamara position and recommended a "measure of defense" for the
country.
February: The Soviet Union announced that it had developed an ABM system capable of protecting it against
attack.
June: The House Appropriations Committee report on
the Department of Defense appropriations bill for fiscal

1968 stated: "It would appear that the initiation of deployment of 'light' or 'thin' defense, now, may very well be a most useful first step toward whatever level of ballistic missile defense ultimately appears necessary."

A hydrogen bomb was detonated by the Chinese.

At the Glassboro Conference President Johnson declared his hope to work with the Soviet Union in limiting development of strategic nuclear weapons, including ABM systems.

Mid-1967

The fiscal 1968 military budget, containing a total of $782.9 million for anti-ballistic missiles, was approved by the 90th Congress. Of these funds, $297.6 million was allocated for ABM procurement, $421.3 million for ABM research and development, and $64 million for ABM construction. Of this amount, $366 million was specified for the Sentinel system, an allocation that President Johnson requested in anticipation of a decision to deploy.

Heated controversy over the question of ABM deployment developed in Congressional debate over appropriations for fiscal 1968.

September 17: Secretary of Defense McNamara announced the decision to deploy a light ABM system as a deterrent to an expected Chinese ICBM capability in mid-1970.

November: The Defense Department announced that the ABM system to be deployed (named Sentinel) was a portion of the Nike-X system, and identified the first ten areas to be surveyed as possible site locations.

1968

March: President Johnson indicated that the Sentinel program was of the highest national priority.

April: In opening debate on the Defense Department appropriations bill for fiscal 1969 the Senate rejected, by a vote of 28–31, an amendment to delay deployment of the ABM until certified as "practicable" by the Secretary of Defense.

June 24: The Senate rejected by a vote of 34–52 an amendment to delay ABM construction funds for one year.

June 28: Soviet Foreign Minister Gromyko announced Soviet willingness to engage in talks with the United States about strategic arms limitations: "The Soviet Union is ready to enter an exchange of opinions . . . [on] the mutual limitation and later reduction of strategic weapons, both offensive and defensive, including anti-ballistic missiles."

June 29: House debate on portions of the Defense Appropriations Act for fiscal 1969 rejected an amendment to delete acquisition of property and construction of related ABM facilities; 37–106.

August 1: A Senate amendment to delete all funds for ABM construction was rejected, 27–46.

August 20: The Russian invasion of Czechoslovakia served to jeopardize proposed arms control talks and stimulated pressure for ABM deployment in United States.

September 5: Secretary of Defense Clark M. Clifford directed that the ABM system be exempt from the expenditures reduction program.

October 7: The Senate rejected, by a 25–45 roll-call vote, a proposal to delay construction of Sentinel for one year.

Appendix VI

Congress Debates the ABM, 1968

The long-standing Congressional controversy over construction of an anti-ballistic-missile system came to a showdown in the debates of the spring and summer of 1968. At issue were the several Department of Defense appropriations bills for fiscal 1969 containing ABM appropriations in the following amounts:

$1,195,600,000	for Sentinel and other anti-missile defenses, including
227,300,000	for construction of ABM facilities
342,700,000	for procurement of Spartan missiles
312,900,000	for research and development of the Sentinel
268,000,000	for testing of other ABM systems such as Nike-X and Defender Radar
44,700,000	for operation, maintenance, and personnel

Save for the allotted $312,900,000 for research and development, ABM opponents mounted their attack on each of the items in five debates and one extraordinary closed session of the Senate.

Three bills were at issue: the Military Procurement Authorization Bill (S 3293), the Military Construction Authorization Bill (HR 16703), and the Military Construction Appropriations Bill (HR 18785).

The final debate took place in the Senate on October 2, 1968. Edited speeches from the floor by Senator John Sherman Cooper (R., Ky.), a leader of the opposition, and Senator J. Strom Thurmond (R., S.C.), who summarizes the proponents' position, are reproduced.

A record of the Senate vote on the final debate concludes Appendix A.

A. The Congressional Challenges

of ABM Opponents

April 18, 1968—(*S 3293*): Senator John Sherman Cooper (R., Ky.) led the opposition attempt to delete $342,700,000 for Sentinel procurement and to delay deployment.

AMENDMENTS:

1. to delete all procurement funds (Senator Gaylord Nelson, D., Wis.)
   Rejected: 17–41 roll-call vote
2. to delay deployment until the Sentinel system is certified as "practicable" and its "costs are known with reasonable accuracy" (Senator John S. Cooper)
   Rejected: 28–31 roll-call vote

June 24, 1968—(HR 16703):

AMENDMENTS:

1. to delay for a year the $227,300,000 designated for construction of ABM facilities (Senator John Sherman Cooper, R., Ky., and Senator Philip A. Hart, D., Mich.)
   Rejected: 34–52 roll-call vote
2. to delete entire ABM authorization (Senator Stephen M. Young, D., Ohio)
   Rejected: 12–72 roll-call vote

July 11, 1968—(S 3293): When the defense procurement authorization reached the House floor, an amendment to delete the $342,700,000 for ABM procurement was offered (Rep. Robert L. Leggett, D., Calif.)
Rejected: 40–147 standing vote

July 29, 1968—(HR 16703): An amendment was offered to remove the full $263,300,000 for acquisition of property and construction of related facilities (Rep. Jeffrey Cohelan, D., Calif.)
Rejected: 37–106 standing vote

August 1, 1968—(HR 18707): An amendment was offered to delete all funds for construction (Senator Gaylord Nelson, D., Wis.)
Rejected: 27–46 roll-call vote

October 2, 1968—(*Department of Defense Appropriations, 1969*): A final effort by ABM opponents to delay construction for one year was deferred following an extraordinary closed session.

AMENDMENT:

to block ABM deployment by deleting $387,400,000 in Sentinel procurement, personnel, and operating funds, leaving in the $312,900,000 for research and development (Senator John Sherman Cooper, R., Ky., and Senator Philip A. Hart, D., Mich.)
Rejected: 25–45 roll-call vote

FINAL SENATE VOTE
Defense Appropriations, 1969
October 2, 1968

[No. 303 Leg.]
YEAS—25

Brooke
Case
Clark
Cooper
Fulbright
Goodell
Gore
Gruening
Hart

Hatfield
Inouye
Kennedy
Mansfield
Metcalf
Moss
Pell
Percy
Prouty

Proxmire
Randolph
Scott
Symington
Tydings
Williams, N.J.
Young, Ohio

NAYS—45

Allott
Anderson
Baker
Boggs
Burdick
Byrd, Va.
Byrd, W. Va.
Cannon
Carlson
Curtis
Dirksen
Dodd
Dominick
Eastland
Ervin

Fong
Griffin
Hansen
Harris
Hayden
Hickenlooper
Hill
Holland
Hruska
Jackson
Jordan, Idaho
Kuchel
Lausche
Long, La.
Magnuson

McClellan
McIntyre
Miller
Montoya
Mundt
Pastore
Pearson
Russell
Sparkman
Spong
Stennis
Talmadge
Thurmond
Williams, Del.
Young, N. Dak.

NOT VOTING—30

Aiken
Bartlett
Bayh
Bennett
Bible
Brewster
Church
Cotton
Ellender
Fannin

Hartke
Hollings
Javits
Jordan, N.C.
Long, Mo.
McCarthy
McGee
McGovern
Mondale
Monroney

Morse
Morton
Murphy
Muskie
Nelson
Ribicoff
Smathers
Smith
Tower
Yarborough

APPENDIX VI

B. SPEECH BY

THE HON. JOHN SHERMAN COOPER,

UNITED STATES SENATOR, REPUBLICAN, KENTUCKY

From the debate of October 2, 1968, during consideration of Department of Defense Appropriations, 1969.

I believe, as do my colleagues who have joined with me . . . that before we take . . . an irreversible step toward the deployment of this [Sentinel] system . . . that we should fully examine its purpose. According to the Administration, it is supposed to be directed against an alleged Chinese threat. Yet it is generally considered by the Administration as the commencement of a heavy ABM system directed against the Soviet threat.

Once the Sentinel system is deployed, it will be difficult . . . ever to reverse a full ABM deployment. We will have committed the nation to the expenditure of over $5 billion on the so-called thin system against the Chinese threat. More accurately, I believe, we will have entered upon an expenditure of from $40 billion to $70 billion or more toward the development of a system designed to meet a Soviet threat, a system which will have the effect of causing the Soviets to erect a similar system. Ultimately, no advantage will accrue to either the United States or the Soviet Union when the systems are completed.

The seriousness of this issue cannot be stated in terms of money . . . . The true issue is whether the installation of an ABM system—a thin system against a Chinese threat or against a Soviet threat—will increase the security of the United States and protect our people. Or will it lead to the installation of a system of vast cost which would be matched by the Soviets? The consequences of deployment at last would bring no additional protection and only an increase in nuclear weapons and an enlargement of the danger of nuclear disaster.

Several propositions . . . argued strongly by the proponents of the ABM system . . . need closer examination. Attention [should be focused first on] the proposition that it is necessary to provide funds for a thin system against a Communist Chinese nuclear threat.

Is Sentinel a Defense Against Chinese Missile Threat?

The Communist Chinese have not yet fired an ICBM missile, but it is only fair to say that it is expected that . . . [they] would be able to fire a number of missiles against the United States by the mid-seventies. The number of such missiles . . . is classified, but from statements by former Secretary of Defense McNamara and others, it appears that the estimate is under ten missiles. Witnesses have stated that if the United States deploys the thin system, the Chinese would not be foolish enough to develop a hardened missile with aids to enable it to penetrate the thin system. It is also admitted . . . that as the Chinese develop larger numbers and more effective missiles, the United States would be required to "heavy" its thin system. Senator Russell expressed what I believe to be a logical view when he said in the course of the hearings that he did not believe the Chinese were crazy enough "to attack us with four or five missiles when they know we have the capability of virtually destroying their entire country." The argument for a thin missile system rests, I submit, on thin ground.

SENATOR COOPER: *Is it the case that this proposal to install the so-called thin system was not one really directed against a Chinese threat, but against a threat from the Soviet Union?*
SENATOR RUSSELL: *It was my view that this system could of course be used against any Chinese threat, but I considered it to be—and I want to be frank with the Senator and not deceive*

anyone—the foundation stone of a missile system to protect us against missiles of the Soviet Union . . . and the beginning of a system to protect . . . this country against a Soviet missile atomic attack.*

Sentinel Is Directed Against Soviet Threat

It has become clear . . . that the Joint Chiefs of Staff and the Senators who are . . . influential in military affairs consider and intend that the thin Sentinel system be the first installation of a heavier system oriented against an attack by the Soviet Union. I quote from page 612, Volume 2, of the hearings held in May by the Appropriations Committee:

SENATOR STENNIS: *It is my understanding that the Joint Chiefs of Staff still recommend the development of an ABM system to protect against a Soviet missile attack. Is this correct?*

GENERAL JOHNSON: *Yes. In addressing actions on force levels, the Joint Chiefs of Staff have stated that "none is more necessary for the defense of the United States than the deployment of an effective ballistic missile defense against the Soviet Union."*

SENATOR STENNIS: *[Is it correct] that elements of the Sentinel system would serve as the first increments to the deployment of a system to defend against the Russian threat?*

GENERAL JOHNSON: *Yes. The Sentinel system as approved for deployment is considered to be a worthwhile initial step toward an effective defense against the Russian threat.*

The . . . chairman of the Armed Services Committee, Senator Russell, has made it plain that in his view the Sentinel is directed against the Soviet Union and not against Communist China. In May, before the Appropriations Committee during a discussion with General Starbird, director of the Sentinel program, he said:

* From the Senate's closed hearings on ABM, October 2, 1968.

SENATOR RUSSELL: *This concept of a missile attack originating in China . . . seems to me to be very remote . . . . All of this talk about preparing for a Chinese missile attack, in my judgment, is just to cover up an admission of error in not starting an anti-ballistic-missile system against Soviet Russia any earlier than we did.*

Later, in the same testimony, Senator Russell said:

It is inconceivable to me that they would fire the first ones they had against this country and know they would be destroyed if they did so. I am glad we are going ahead, you understand, but I don't like people to think that I am being kidded by this talk of defense against a Chinese nuclear threat because I don't think that the Chinese are likely to attack us with an intercontinental ballistic missile at any time in the near future . . . .
I'm delighted that the executive branch finally decided to proceed with the deployment of even this thin ABM system, because it is the first step toward the deployment of the complete system that I think is required.

I   agree with Senator Russell and Senator Stennis that the true purpose of [Sentinel] is to commence the installation of an anti-Soviet system.

The Nature and Status of Soviet ABM Deployment

Undoubtedly the pressures that have built up . . . for deployment of an ABM system are due to concern for the Soviet deployment of a defense system at Moscow and perhaps at Tallinn. We must inquire as to the kind of ABM systems the Soviets have been installing . . . and whether [they] would affect the capacity of our offensive missile system to destroy the Soviet Union even if it should first attack the United States.
Reliable sources of intelligence [have detailed] first, the so-called Leningrad system is obsolete and does not exist in any effective form; second, . . . the weight of authority is that the

so-called Tallinn system is directed against aircraft and air-breathing missiles; third, the Moscow system has been reduced in size and number of its components, and its installation has been measurably slowed down; and fourth, the existing system at Moscow could be destroyed by our offensive nuclear weapons.

SENATOR COOPER: Senator Russell has emphasized that an ABM system is being deployed around Moscow. The report of the Senate Preparedness Subcommittee states: "The system may now have a limited operations capability, but the slow pace of development and the fact that it has not been deployed at other cities probably indicates that Soviet officials have reservations about its effectiveness." Is it not correct that this system around Moscow has been slowed down?

SENATOR RUSSELL: The Soviets have reduced the content of their anti-missile complex around Moscow . . . . It could well be that the Soviets have encountered some difficulties in the development of their missiles. That is nothing new. We have had all kinds of trouble with ours, and we have had to rebuild and remake them from time to time. . . . I did not think their scientists were any better than ours, and it turned out they were not any better. I think they are having all kinds of trouble.*

The argument that the experience the Soviet Union has gained in the installation of its works around Moscow has provided them with a dangerous lead must be looked at from the standpoint of the relative effectiveness of the partially deployed Soviet system and the system the United States has the capacity to deploy. . . . Our intelligence says that the components of the Moscow system are inferior to those being developed by the United States. The United States has developed and is testing some of the components of the Sentinel system; and further tests are scheduled, and components yet to be built are being developed. Because of our research and development, if it should become necessary to install an ABM

* From the Senate's closed hearings of October 2, 1968.

system, ours would be superior to that now installed in the Soviet Union.

Is there danger in postponing the initiation of the Sentinel system . . . ? The United States can at any time destroy the Soviet system now deployed around Moscow. Our nuclear arsenal consists of over 1,700 ICBM's on land sites and under the sea. Our SAC Air Force carries an even vaster destructive force. This missile force, it is said, will be increased by a factor of five to ten times by the development of MIRV—multiple independently targetable re-entry vehicles. In addition, we have approximately 7,000 nuclear weapons of various ranges in Europe.

Senator Joseph Clark: *Does the Senator know of anything which has developed in the last year which would question the conclusion that today we could destroy Moscow in a matter of hours and they could destroy Washington or New York in a matter of hours, and there would be tens of millions of casualties?*

Senator Russell: *There is no question that we could destroy Moscow, not in a matter of hours, but in a matter of minutes, and they could destroy Washington, New York and Philadelphia in a matter of minutes.*

Senator Clark: *There is nothing in this defense system which would stop it.**

The history of the nuclear arms race is one of action by the United States or the Soviet Union, of reaction and counter reactions. Every intelligence estimate considers that if the United States builds an effective Sentinel system, it will only lead to the installation of a similar system by the Soviet Union. Every civilian and military authority has declared publicly that the United States has the capacity of assured destruction—that is, the ability to destroy the Soviet Union even if it should first attack the United States. And they agree that the Soviet Union has the same capacity to destroy the United States. If this is correct, the construction of a Soviet ABM system would not

* From the Senate's closed hearings of October 2, 1968.

degrade our assured ability to destroy the Soviet Union. Correspondingly, the Sentinel ABM system, thick or thin, will not alter the capacity of the Soviet Union to destroy the United States.

Will ABM Deployment Save Lives?

An argument made again and again . . . is that we must install the ABM system to save the lives of our people. [Two assumptions lie behind this argument]: one, that the system deployed would provide an effective defense against Soviet offensive missiles; and two, that if the United States installs a heavy ABM system, the U.S.S.R. would not do so. Every statement by those in authority negates this argument [by declaring] that the Soviet Union would react and would install a similar system. Secretary McNamara has provided estimates of the lives that would be lost in both the United States and the Soviet Union [in the event of a nuclear showdown]. The table shows that if the United States deployed a heavy ballistic-missile system against the Soviet Union and the Soviet Union then deployed a system, the ultimate result would be that the number of lives lost would be about the same, no matter who struck first. Secretary McNamara's table indicates that after both had deployed such systems, the lives lost would be comparably the same as if neither had installed a system.

SENATOR RUSSELL: The question is, How many [missiles] can we knock down and how many lives can we save in this country? We are never going to have an absolute, impregnable defense against missiles either from China, from Russia, or from any other missile-producing country capable of producing an atomic warhead.

I stress that we can save the lives of millions of people, but we will have no absolute foolproof defense—I do not care how much money we spend on one or what we do.

Senator [Joseph] Clark calls upon former Secretary McNa-

NUMBERS OF FATALITIES IN AN ALL-OUT STRATEGIC
EXCHANGE, MID-1970's *

U.S. program	Soviet response	Soviets strike first against military and city targets; United States retaliates against cities		United States strikes first at military targets; Soviets retaliate against U.S. cities and United States retaliates against Soviet cities	
		U.S. fatalities (in millions)	Soviet fatalities (in millions)	U.S. fatalities (in millions)	Soviet fatalities (in millions)
No ABM	None	120	120	120	80
Sentinel	do	100	120	90	80
	Pen-Aids	120	120	110	80
Posture A	None	40	120	10	80
	MIRV, Pen-Aids	110	120	60	80
	Plus 100 mobile ICBM's	110	120	90	80
Posture B	None	20	120	10	80
	MIRV, Pen-Aids	70	120	40	80
	Plus 550 mobile ICBM's	100	120	90	80

* At fatality levels approximating 100,000,000 or more, differences of 10,000,000 to 20,000,000 in the calculated results are less than the margin of error in the estimates.

mara as an authority. Everybody knows how he went into these matters. His analysis showed that even a thin system could save many millions of American lives.

SENATOR CLARK: He said that only after some thirty or forty million Americans had been killed.

SENATOR RUSSELL: But that is not to say that if we cannot save them all, we want to see them all killed. Is that the Senator's position?

SENATOR CLARK: There comes a time when the tens of millions of casualties are so enormous that civilization is destroyed, and if there are a few people living in caves after that, it does not make much difference.

SENATOR RUSSELL: If we have to start over again with another Adam and Eve, then I want them to be Americans and not Russians, and I want them on this continent and not in Europe.*

ABM Deployment and Arms Control

The Senate has been asked to ratify the Nuclear Nonproliferation Treaty. The treaty has as its chief object the prevention of the proliferation of nuclear weapons by binding non-nuclear-weapons nations from ever developing or possessing nuclear weapons. In turn, the nuclear nations are bound by Article VI "to pursue negotiations in good faith on effective measures relating to cessation of the nuclear arms race."

The Senate, on May 12, 1966, approved these objectives:

Resolved, That the Senate commends the President's serious and urgent efforts to negotiate international agreements limiting the spread of nuclear weapons and supports the principle of additional efforts by the President which are appropriate and necessary in the interest of peace and for the solution of nuclear proliferation problems.

President Johnson and before him President Truman, President Eisenhower, and President Kennedy, have sought enforceable agreements with the Soviet Union on the control of nuclear weapons. President Johnson proposed again last year negotiations with the Soviet Union, and only recently [June, 1968] the Soviet Union signified its willingness to enter into negotiations on the limitations of offensive and defensive nuclear weapons.

No one can say whether there will be negotiations or whether agreements will be reached. I believe that it is reasonable to delay the deployment of this new nuclear weapons system for at least a year, to determine whether the Soviet Union will enter into meaningful negotiations.

Let us not, when there is a chance to bring reason to the

* From the Senate's closed hearings of October 2, 1968.

world and a halt to the mad momentum of the nuclear race, jeopardize the chance we need, the world needs, by the wrong decision. The correct decision, the hard decision, the tough decision, in my view, is to delay the deployment of the Sentinel system and pursue negotiations with the Soviets on defensive and offensive weapons. What we may be able to gain is a way to lessen the dangers of nuclear disaster, a way toward security and the protection of our people, and, in truth, the protection of civilization.

So the real question, as I see it, is whether we can delay for one year, to then determine if the Soviet Union does continue with its deployment of the system around Moscow or any other place in the Soviet Union; and whether we should take the chance and admit there is just a possibility that the efforts which have been made toward negotiation with the Soviet Union will be fruitful in order to see if there can be some halt to the proliferation of these weapons.

In Summation

My argument for postponing all deployment of the system is simply: The system itself, if it is deployed—even a thin system —would not give protection against even a limited Chinese threat. It would give no protection at all against the Soviet threat. If the system is installed, the Soviets will match our system with a similar system; and both the United States and the Soviet Union will be able to build defense missiles which will penetrate our ABM system. The Chinese have the technological capability to do so as well. And, in the end, we will be in the same relative position that we are in now, except that there will have been an expenditure of forty to seventy billion dollars. And we will have filled the land and choked the earth with more and more nuclear weapons.

C. Speech by The Hon. J. Strom Thurmond,

United States Senator,

Republican, South Carolina

> From the debate of October 2,
> 1968, during consideration of De-
> partment of Defense Appropria-
> tions, 1969.

It is disturbing to see this important advance in our defense
system once again become the subject of controversy. When
Soviet tanks rumbled across Czechoslovakia, I should have
thought that perceptive observers of international political realities would see the futility of a defense policy based in its essence
on the good intentions of the Soviet Union. I would have
thought that the saber-rattling statements of the Soviet leaders
attempting to justify some future military thrust into West
Germany under the guise of stemming the rebirth of militarism
would have dealt an additional blow to the concept of weakening our own defense in order to persuade our Soviet enemy of
our peaceful intentions. Yet we have seen that 250 Czechoslova-
kians are not yet cold in their graves when once again we are
asked to impede, to slow down, and to weaken our own defense
capability.

I was pleased with the statement of Defense Secretary Clark
Clifford on September 5 that our anti-ballistic-missile program
would be exempt from any Pentagon budget cuts. It is high
time that the American people and the members of this body
recognize the serious state of our defense capability.

The deployment of the Sentinel system to defend our military installations and some of our cities against the possibility of
an ICBM attack from the Chinese People's Republic is directly
related to the future security of this country.

Threat from China and Russia

The best authorities from the Defense Intelligence Agency and from the Army testified to the committee's satisfaction that the Red Chinese ICBM development is a definite threat. At the same time they revealed alarming changes in the over-all strategic balance between the United States and the Soviet Union. Our military advisers told us that one of the greatest advantages from the installation of the Sentinel is that it will establish a base which could be expanded in a relatively short time to a more comprehensive, larger system for use against the Soviet threat if it is required.

Sentinel Requires Testing

I would like to point out that the Sentinel system is a very complex system which will take time to establish, to bring it into an operational readiness status, to test all the components, and to establish with some degree of competence what we can and cannot do with it. Regardless of any delays that might be experienced by our enemies, the fact remains that it is unwise to concentrate on and rely too much on a single system for the future security of the United States. Should we conclude that an adequate offensive nuclear strategic weapon capability will guarantee our security, we would be overlooking one of the more important elements of the problem. If the Soviets develop a capable anti-missile defense, and there is every indication that they are doing so, then our calculations on the capability of our offensive weapons will not be valid.

As the Committee on Armed Services sees the problem, this is not a question of arms control or nuclear power; this is a case of the Soviets building a defense against our strategic-weapon delivery systems while we do nothing but research.

Arguments for Sentinel Deployment

I should like to summarize the main arguments for proceeding promptly with the development of the Sentinel ABM system:

First. This is a very complex system. The Army needs every opportunity to test the equipment, and it needs a base from which to begin. Even with good results it will take approximately four years to make the Sentinel system operational.

Second. If there is some delay in Red Chinese development of an ICBM, we should take advantage of the additional time gained to iron out difficulties and perfect the Sentinel system.

Third. The Sentinel will not only defend against an ICBM attack by Red China, but also it will provide the United States with protection against an accidental or irrational ICBM launch by any power.

Fourth. The capability provided by Sentinel will discourage nuclear proliferation among lesser powers.

Fifth. Acting on good faith, on the DOD decision announced by Secretary McNamara and subsequently reaffirmed by Secretary Clifford, the Army has let contracts, hired people, and formed technical teams to get the Sentinel project moving.

Sixth. The Army needs to break ground and start construction. Any delay in establishing these sites will cause a whiplash in the development of other essential components. In other words, delay in construction will snowball other delays.

Seventh. To those who object to Sentinel development on the grounds that we cannot test the system completely, I point out that neither can we test Minuteman or Polaris in that context. To those who now argue against Sentinel on that basis, I ask, How did they vote on the Nuclear Test-Ban Treaty of 1963?

Eighth. I should like to point out the growth capacity of the Sentinel system. While it is admittedly oriented against the Red Chinese threat, it also has a capability against the more dangerous threat of the Soviet Union. Additional faces can be added to the missile site radars and the perimeter acquisition radars to give wider coverage and expand the capability of the Sentinel.

Ninth. The Sentinel would provide protection against accidental missile launch from any nation, and as I have stated, it would provide increased defense of our Minuteman and other strategic forces, including our strategic bomber bases.

On June 18, 1968, Secretary Clark Clifford wrote the Senator from Georgia [Mr. Russell], the chairman of the Armed Services Committee, a letter on this subject.*

Dear Senator Russell:

You asked that I give you my personal views with respect to proceeding with the deployment of the Sentinel Antiballistic Missile System.

During the three and a half months since I became Secretary of Defense, I have had an opportunity to go into the merits of the System in considerable depth. As a result of that review I have come to the conclusion that it would be a serious mistake to eliminate construction and procurement funds in fiscal year 1969 for the deployment of the Sentinel System.

The reasons for that view are the following. The program represents twelve years of intense research and development effort. During those years we have devoted a substantial portion of our best scientific technological abilities to its development at a cost of some $3 billion. As long as seven years ago we demonstrated that we could with confidence destroy single incoming missiles. Since that time we have demonstrated that we can reliably track substantial numbers of incoming objects and defend the U.S. from relatively simple missile attacks. I believe that the time has arrived when we can no longer rely merely on continued research and development but should proceed with actual deployment of an operating system.

The Director of Defense Research and Engineering, Dr. John Foster, has prepared the following statement of the purposes

* Senator Clifford's letter to Senator Russell, having been frequently cited by proponents of Sentinel, is reprinted in full at the editor's discretion and with due apologies to the Senator.

of the Sentinel System, which I have approved on the recommendation of the Joint Chiefs of Staff and the Secretaries of the Army, Navy and the Air Force.

"The Sentinel missile defense system is designed to (a) prevent a successful missile attack from China through the late 1970's (with the capability to continue to deny or at least substantially reduce damage from threats in later years); (b) limit damage from an accidental launch from any source; and (c) provide the option for increased defense of our Minuteman force, if necessary in the future.

"The ability to protect ourselves from unacceptable damage from a numerically large and technically advanced missile force such as that of the Soviet Union is not yet technically feasible. However the Sentinel system will complicate any attack on the United States.

"We will continue an intensive R&D program in an attempt to provide increasingly effective means to limit damage from both the advancing Chinese and the Soviet missile threats."

I understand that a proposal may be introduced in the Senate to eliminate funds for development of the Sentinel System in fiscal year 1969 and restrict the program to continued research and development. Approval of such a proposal would disrupt the work currently underway and, more seriously, would lose some two years in the availability of an operating system which in my judgment is important to the security of the United States.

I believe that our deployment decision is consistent with our continuing desire for arms control and arms limitation. The Soviets are, at the present time, deploying a ballistic missile defense around Moscow. We will continue our efforts to negotiate limitation of both strategic offensive and defensive weapons systems, but, in the absence of agreement, we must not suspend taking action in our own defense.

I have discussed the above views with the President, who shares my concern.

CLARK M. CLIFFORD

I would just make this point, in his words. He said: "It would be a serious mistake to eliminate construction and procurement funds in fiscal year 1969 for the deployment of the Sentinel System."

Also, I would remind the Senate that the Joint Chiefs of Staff have recommended going ahead with this program. I would further remind the Senate that the Secretaries of the Army, the Navy, and the Air Force favor going ahead with the program. I would remind the Senate that Secretary Clifford, in that letter, said that if we do not go ahead now with a proposal of the kind that is being advanced here, it will "disrupt the work currently underway, and, more seriously, would lose some two years in the availability of an operating system which, in my judgment, is important to the security of the United States."

In the same letter Secretary Clifford made this statement: "The Soviets are, at the present time, deploying a ballistic missile defense around Moscow."

How can we afford not to go ahead when the Soviets have their system already deployed? I repeat, we are four or five years behind now, and we cannot afford to wait. Some people have said this system is unproved. That is untrue. We have been doing research on the system for about twelve years. We have spent three billion dollars doing research on the system, and we are ready, now, to go ahead.

In conclusion, I cannot help but remind the Senators who oppose the deployment of Sentinel for economic reasons that the Soviets are not reluctant to make a heavy investment in a similar system. The difference in American and Soviet attitudes towards strategic defense today might well mean victory or defeat in a nuclear showdown tomorrow.

Appendix VII

A Glossary of Strategic Weaponry

ABM (anti-ballistic missile): a missile, or combination of missiles, radar, and data-processing systems designed to intercept and destroy incoming missiles before they reach their intended targets.

Assured Destruction: that level and deployment of U.S. nuclear capability which, as defined by former Secretary of Defense McNamara, serves "to deter deliberate nuclear attack upon the United States and its allies by maintaining, continuously, a highly reliable ability to inflict an unacceptable degree of damage upon any single aggressor, or combination of aggressors, at any time during the course of a strategic nuclear exchange, even after absorbing a surprise first strike."

Atlas: a liquid-fueled U.S. ICBM of the 1950's and early 1960's, subsequently phased out with the advent of solid-propellant long-range missiles.

138

BMEWS (ballistic missile early warning system): a U.S. electronic defense network, based primarily in Greenland and Alaska, established in the early 1960's to give early warning of incoming trans-Arctic missiles.

Damage Limitation (as defined by Secretary Clifford): the ability to reduce the potential damage of a nuclear attack upon the United States through the use of both offensive and defensive weapons.

FOBS (fractional orbit bombardment system): a nuclear delivery system intended to deliver its warhead to a target on the first (fractional) orbit around the earth, rather than on a ballistic trajectory. FOBS would deliver a smaller payload less accurately than an ICBM using the same booster rocket.

Galosh: a Soviet ABM missile system comparable to the U.S. Nike-Zeus, partially deployed around Moscow.

Golem: a Soviet submarine-launched missile of IRBM class.

Griffon: a Soviet short-range, anti-aircraft missile having no ABM capability.

ICBM (intercontinental ballistic missile): a long-range (6,000–8,000 miles) multistage rocket capable of delivering nuclear warheads to enemy targets. U.S. ICBM's include Titan I and II and Minuteman I and II. Soviet ICBM's include Savage, Scrag, and Proton.

IRBM (intermediate-range ballistic missile): a multistage missile with a range of 1,500–2,500 miles. U.S. missiles currently deployed in this category include only those of the Polaris type.

MAR (multifunction array radar): a U.S. detection and command system designed for use with the Nike-X ABM system.

Megaton: a measurement of explosive capability applied to nuclear armaments. One megaton is the equivalent of one million tons of TNT.

Minuteman: the basic U.S. ICBM. Minuteman I yields one megaton, and Minuteman II carries a higher yield and/or trade-off with penetration aids. Minuteman III will be designed to carry MIRV's.

MIRV (multiple independent re-entry vehicle): a system of multiple warheads in which several carried by one ICBM re-entry vehicle can be maneuvered on independent courses to separate targets. MIRV's are being developed by the U.S. and reportedly by the Soviet Union.

MSR (missile-site radar): together with a data-processing subsystem, part of the Sentinel ABM. Performs surveillance and detection, target track, missile track, and command functions for the Spartan and Sprint missiles. Power and detection range are considerably less than those of the PAR; provides refined tracking data and missile command after initial acquisition and tracking by the more powerful PAR.

Nike-X: the thick U.S. ABM system, designed in 1963, utilizing the Sprint missile in combination with the MAR detection system, together with the long range Spartan missile and the PAR detection system.

Nike-Zeus: a U.S. ABM system, authorized in 1957 but never deployed; predecessor to the Nike-X system.

PAR (perimeter acquisition radar): a long-range detection system, one of the five subsystems of the Sentinel ABM. Used as surveillance and tracking radar, primarily in conjunction with the Spartan ABM.

Polaris: the basic U.S. submarine-launched missile with a range of approximately 2,800 miles. Scheduled to be replaced in the 1970's by the Poseidon missile.

Poseidon: a U.S. submarine-launched missile, scheduled to replace Polaris on 31 of the 41 Polaris Submarines and to carry MIRV's.

Sabmis (sea-based anti-ballistic-missile intercept system): a concept proposed for future development by the U.S., involving a network of ABM's situated on surface or submarine vessels and possessing a complete mobility.

SAGE (semi-automatic ground environment): a U.S. defense system that provides instantaneous information for waging air battles.

Sark-Serb: a Soviet submarine-launched IRBM system.

Savage: a Soviet three-stage, solid-propellant ICBM, similar to the U.S. Minuteman, with a range of over 5,000 miles.

Scrag: a combined orbital, sub-orbital, and ballistic system developed by the Soviet Union, comprising a three-stage weapon —an ICBM, a space bomb, or a fractional-orbit weapon.

Sentinel: the so-called light or thin anti-ballistic-missile system being deployed by the U.S. against the possibility of Chinese-launched "primitive" ICBM's.

Spartan: a long-range missile component of the Sentinel ABM system, three-state, solid-propellant, with a nuclear warhead; fired from an underground cell.

Sprint: the short-range missile component of the Sentinel ABM system; a two-stage solid-propellant vehicle designed to deliver a nuclear warhead; fired from an underground vertical launcher, guided by MSR.

Tallinn: a Soviet anti-aircraft defense system having no ABM capabilities, installed around Moscow and Leningrad.

Titan: U.S. liquid-propellant ICBM. The Titan II, with a warhead yield in excess of five megatons, is scheduled for phase-out in 1970, to be replaced by the Minuteman II.

X-ray Effect: an ABM kill mechanism. An effect that neutralizes ICBM guidance equipment at a great distance from the actual intended ABM explosion.

Biographical Notes

HARRY S. ASHMORE is Executive Vice President of the Center for the Study of Democratic Institutions; he has served as a member of the Center's Board of Directors since 1954 and as Chairman of its Executive Committee since 1959. Formerly Executive Editor of the *Arkansas Gazette*, he and his newspaper won the first double Pulitzer Prizes ever granted for distinguished analysis of the Little Rock integration controversy. Editor-in-Chief of *Encyclopaedia Britannica* from 1960 to 1965 and Editor of the *Britannica*'s "Perspectives" series (1968), he is the author of *The Negro and the Schools, An Epitaph for Dixie, The Other Side of Jordan, The Man in The Middle,* and in 1968 wrote, in collaboration with the late William C. Baggs, *Mission to Hanoi.* A Nieman Fellow of Harvard University and personal assistant to Adlai E. Stevenson in the 1956 Presidential campaign, Mr. Ashmore is presently conducting an extended study of electoral reform for the Center.

142

ADOLF A. BERLE is a consultant to the Center for the Study of Democratic Institutions and a partner in the law firm of Berle and Berle. For many years a Professor of Law at Columbia University, he is perhaps better known for the numerous governmental appointments he has held, including that of Assistant Secretary of State, U.S. Ambassador to Brazil, and Director of President Kennedy's Task Force on Latin American Affairs. Among his many books are *The Tides of Crisis* and *The Twentieth Century Capitalist Revolution*.

DONALD G. BRENNAN is a mathematician and student of national security problems. His researches in advanced military policy, arms control, and ballistic-missile defense are conducted at the Hudson Institute, of which he was President from 1962 to 1964. Under the auspices of the American Academy of Sciences he organized in 1958 and in 1960 the Summer Study of Arms Control and was the Chairman of the Academy's Committee on International Studies of Arms Control. A frequent consultant to the Department of State, the Department of Defense, and the Arms Control and Disarmament Agency, he is the Editor of the international journal *Arms Control and Disarmament Annual Review*. A frequent contributor to scholarly journals, he has lectured both at major universities in the United States and at defense study centers in Bonn, Paris, and Oslo.

WILLIAM O. DOUGLAS is an Associate Justice of the United States Supreme Court and Chairman of the Board of Directors of the Center for the Study of Democratic Institutions. Prior to his appointment to the Supreme Court he was Professor of Law at Yale and Columbia universities and served on the Securities and Exchange Commission. A world traveler and inveterate author, his works include *America Challenged, Anatomy of Liberty, Living Bill of Rights,* and *Of Men and Mountains.*

FREEMAN DYSON has been Professor of Physics at the Institute for Advanced Study since 1953. Granted the Ph.D. degree from

Cambridge University, he was Chairman of the Federation of American Scientists from 1962 to 1963 and was elected a member of the National Academy of Sciences in 1964. He is a frequent consultant to the United States government as well as to weapons laboratories, the National Aeronautics and Space Administration, and the United States Arms Control and Disarmament Agency.

W. H. FERRY is a Vice President of the Center for the Study of Democratic Institutions and was director of the Center's colloquy in *Anti-Ballistic Missile: Yes or No?* After serving in 1944 as Director of Public Relations of the CIO Political Action Committee, he was for nine years a partner of Earl Newsom and Company, New York public relations counsel. A contributor to the book *The Corporation Takeover*, he has written several Center studies, among which are *Caught on the Horn of Plenty, Farewell to Integration,* and *Masscomm as Guru.*

CHARLES M. HERZFELD is Technical Director of the Defense-Space Group for International Telephone and Telegraph Corporation and was Director of the Advanced Research Projects Agency in the Department of Defense from 1965 to 1967. The Director of Ballistic Missile Defense for the Department of Defense from 1961 to 1963, he has served as Associate Director of the National Bureau of Standards and was a Professor of Physics at the University of Maryland until 1961. He is a member of the Catholic Association for International Peace, having served as its President from 1959 to 1961.

NEIL H. JACOBY is a Visiting Fellow at the Center for the Study of Democratic Institutions, on leave from the University of California at Los Angeles, where he is Professor of Business Economics and Policy and was Dean of the Graduate School of Business Administration for twenty years. He served as a member of President Eisenhower's Council of Economic Advisers from 1953 to 1955 and as the United States Representative in the Economic and Social Council of the United Nations in 1957.

LEON W. JOHNSON, General, U.S.A.F. (retired), is a specialist in strategic studies, serving as a consultant to the TEMPO division of General Electric and the Strategic Study Center of the Stanford Research Institute. During the Berlin airlift he was the Commander of United States Air Forces in England and was Air Force Representative to the United States Mission to the United Nations from 1953 to 1956, United States Representative to the Military Committee of NATO from 1956 to 1958, and in 1961 Director of the Net Evaluation Sub-Committee of the United States Security Council with special responsibilities to the Strategic Field.

DONALD McDONALD is a Fellow of the Center for the Study of Democratic Institutions. From 1962 to 1965 the Dean of the College of Journalism, Marquette University, he is author of a syndicated column, "Essays in Our Day," for the Catholic Press. From 1964 to 1965 he served as Director of the Center for the Study of the American Press and in 1958 wrote *Religion and Freedom* for the Fund for the Republic's seminar, "Religion in a Free Society." Having conducted a series of interviews for the Center's "Study of the American Character," he is presently engaged in extensive studies of the military-industrial complex.

GEORGE S. McGOVERN has been United States Senator from South Dakota since 1963. A former professor of history and government, he was elected to the U.S. House of Representatives in 1956 and 1958 and was U.S. Delegate to the NATO Parliamentarians Conference in 1958 and 1959. Director of the Food for Peace program and Special Assistant to President Kennedy in 1961, he presently serves on the Senate Committees of Agriculture and Forestry, and Interior and Insular Affairs, being Chairman of the Subcommittee on Indian Affairs. A leading Senate critic of anti-ballistic-missile deployment, he is the editor of *Agriculture Policy in The Twentieth Century* and the author of *War Against Want* and most recently *A Time of War: A Time of Peace*.

I. I. RABI is a consultant to the Center for the Study of Democratic Institutions, University Professor of Physics at Columbia University, and Nobel laureate in physics, 1944. The recipient of innumerable honorary degrees and awards granted by universities and governments in Europe and the Western Hemisphere, his distinguished governmental and international service has included: Chairman of the General Advisory Committee of the Atomic Energy Commission, 1952 to 1956; Vice President of the International Conference on Peaceful Uses of Atomic Energy, 1955, 1958, 1964; Chairman of the President's Science Advisory Committee, 1957; member of the United Nations Science Committee since 1954; and since 1962 member of the General Advisory Committee to the Arms Control and Disarmament Agency. A frequent contributor to scholarly journals, he is the author of *My Life and Time as a Physicist*.

H. FRANZ SCHURMANN is Professor of History and Sociology at the University of California at Berkeley and was Director of the Center for Chinese Studies of The Institute of International Studies for the year 1966 to 1967. Lecturer in Sociology and Near East Languages at California since 1956, Fulbright scholar from 1952 to 1953, and Ford Foundation Fellow from 1952 to 1954, Professor Schurmann has been an outspoken critic of United States involvement in the war in Vietnam. Frequent contributor to scholarly journals, he is the author of several monographs on Chinese history and culture, including *Ideology and Organization in Communist China* and *Politics of Escalation in Vietnam*, and is the co-editor, with Orville Schell, of *China Reader* (3 volumes).

HARVEY WHEELER is a Fellow at the Center for the Study of Democratic Institutions, where he is presently engaged in a comprehensive study, "The Constitutionalization of Science."

A Professor of Political Science at Washington and Lee University, he taught at Harvard and Johns Hopkins universities after serving in military government in the European theater during World War II. The author of several Center publications, including *Restoration of Politics, The Rise and Fall of Liberal Democracy,* and *The Politics of Revolution,* and a frequent contributor to the scholarly journals, he was co-author, with the late Eugene Burdick, of the novel *Fail-Safe* and in 1968 published *Democracy in a Revolutionary Era.*

JEROME B. WIESNER became Provost of the Massachusetts Institute of Technology after serving as Special Assistant for Science and Technology to President Kennedy from 1961 to 1964. A former Director of the Research Laboratory of Electronics at M.I.T., he became a member of the President's Science Advisory Committee in 1957 and served as the first Director of the Office of Science and Technology from 1962 to 1964. A participant in numerous international conferences devoted to disarmament, in 1956 he served as Staff Director of the American delegation to the Geneva Conference for the Prevention of Surprise Attack. A frequent contributor to a wide variety of journals, he is the author of the book *Where Science and Politics Meet.*